"There Is One Leader and You Are ... Not It is destined to become a classic for those wanting to lead in business and life God's way. What you will learn is revolutionary and transform your business, your family and your life."

HOWARD DAYTON
Founder of Compass, Co-founder of Crown Financial Ministries

"I first knew Bruce Witt in Houston years ago when he accepted Jesus Christ as Savior and Lord. It has been a joy to see him grow in his faith as a key leader in our community and church here in Atlanta. His insight on leadership will be helpful to all."

BRYANT WRIGHT
Former President of the Southern Baptist Convention
Sr. Pastor of Johnson Ferry Baptist Church, Marietta, GA

"I have enjoyed a lengthy friendship with Bruce Witt. Based on my experience with him I can affirm that he is an authentic exemplar of the rich principles he develops in his new leadership book. This book unpacks the biblical secret to authentic leadership—the life of the indwelling Christ and the expression of that life through the spiritual growth of the follower of Jesus. Bruce shows that as we draw our vitality from Jesus we will be secure enough to serve and influence the people God has entrusted us with in our relational spheres."

DR. KEN BOA
Author, Speaker, and President of Reflections Ministries

"Bruce Witt models what he talks about, as over the past 22 years in our relationship he always points me back to Jesus. His new book is not just intriguing concepts and interesting theology, but it is a practical guide to lead from Jesus. Read this book about becoming a leader and be blessed immensely."

BOYD BAILEY
President, National Christian Foundation Georgia

"What a refreshing biblical reminder for all leaders. Jesus is our leader and our level of influence is not based on our performance but rather on Him living through us. AMEN!"

ERIK CHRISTENSON
Senior Pastor of Hoffmantown Church, Albuquerque, NM

D0167149

"Any successful leader knows the cost of leadership can be great. Bruce introduces the premise that it is not about refining your great leadership skills and talents. True leadership requires you being led and empowered by the greatest leader of all, Jesus."

RANDALL W. HATCHER
President, MAU, Inc.

"This book is more about who Jesus is than about leadership. And, the theme of the book that leadership flows out of the person of Christ is Biblically and theologically grounded. As someone who has observed the development of the book over the years, it speaks a volume about the heart and passion of the writer. This book does not attempt to teach but guides the reader into being true disciple who would be able to lead from Christ."

SAM Y. HWANG
President, Hwang & Haas, PC
Senior, Pastor, Christ Life Church, Plymouth Meeting, PA
Chairman, Board of Directors, CBMC, Inc.

"Bruce has captured in his book what captured him years ago which is that Christ is our life as believers. He is our everything and apart from Him we are nothing. As we learn to follow Him by daily surrendering our lives to Him and to His Word people will follow us. A true Christian leader is a follower of Christ!"

WAYNE A. BARBER
Senior Pastor of Woodland Park Baptist Church, Chattanooga, TN

"This is the most unique approach to leadership I've seen published. Bruce is taking us back to the ultimate leader and giving us tools to be led by Him. Set aside your prejudice and dive in here. You might just find yourself more effective and useful to God than ever before."

REGI CAMPBELL
Entrepreneur, Founder of Radical Mentoring,
Author of About My Father's Business *and* Mentor like Jesus

THERE IS ONE LEADER AND YOU ARE... NOT IT!

IGNITING A POWERFUL LEADERSHIP REVOLUTION

BRUCE R. WITT

ISBN 978-0-9825332-6-0

Copy Editing and Interior Layout: James Armstrong, Upwrite Publishing
Cover Design: Michael Sean Allen

Leadership Revolution, Inc.
Bruce Witt, President
4465 Nassau Way
Marietta, GA 30068

678-637-9890
Bruce@LeadershipRevolution.us
www.LeadershipRevolution.us

TABLE OF CONTENTS

THERE IS ONE LEADER AND YOU ARE...NOT IT!

INTRODUCTION

To be a better leader, you need a different starting point—a new source of power. Your career, your ministry, and your success will rise and fall on your leadership of others. Your leadership isn't just for gain or outcome, but it's to inspire and transform teams to achieve success.

The only reason that this book will transform your leadership and your life is because it directs your focus to the one true Leader, Jesus Christ! Understanding and following His example of leadership will forever change your leadership thinking and actions. You will experience a new freedom and energy to fulfill God's purpose for your life. Your vision will be clarified and you'll be empowered to equip your team and colleagues.

Here are just two outcomes that the seven spiritual principles outlined in this book have produced in other parts of the world—

> *"I would like to thank you for the dynamic teaching regarding the One Leader that God has entrusted in your hand. Truly speaking, the One Leader Seminar has changed my spiritual life. It gave me a wonderful leadership views and also it gave me new thoughts to equip the real Christian leaders. I came to know that Christ is the Leader and I am a partaker of His work, because He is the source of Leadership."*
>
> Rev. Mark Pani,
> State Coordinator,
> Orissa State, East India

"The One Leader conference has changed my view about leadership. I have learned to release Christ and His power. Before the training my mindset was different and I used to try to do things instead of releasing Christ through my life."

Bro. Thomas Pechak,
Director, East and
North East India

"The voice of the Lord strikes with bolts of lightning" (Psalm 29:7 NLT).

The uniqueness of the principles in this book are represented by an image of a lightning bolt. Consider the characteristics of just one bolt of lightning:

- Its temperature is 50,000 degrees F.
- It has the intensity of 200,000,000 volts or more.
- Its velocity is one third the speed of light.
- It possesses fantastic power focused on a single point.

The ultimate goal of *There is One Leader and...You Are Not It!* is to experience the life and power of Jesus Christ working through us as leaders. This belief and perspective is far different from trying harder, working smarter, or mustering up more energy and more skills.

Just as lightning is a release of power from heaven to earth, so the One Leader releases the power of Christ to make a global and an eternal difference.

Please enjoy this book, and as you read, take action to possess and focus on a new power that can transform your leadership. This is not a method, a program, or simply more principles. It is the supernatural work of God as He uses you in His eternal purposes.

BW

Section One

LAYING THE FOUNDATION FOR THE ONE LEADER

Chapter One

THE CRY OF THE HEART – A WORLD IN NEED

"The American church is dying due to a lack of strong leadership. In this time of unprecedented opportunity and plentiful resources, the American Church is actually losing influence. The primary reason is the lack of leadership. Nothing is more important than leadership."

George Barna[1]

EVERYONE WANTS TO BE A LEADER

The popular buzzword making the rounds through today's organizational and corporate spheres is *leadership*. Leadership books and seminars are everywhere. It seems everyone wants to be a leader. Why? Leadership brings success, rank, and prestige. Leaders are looked up to; they are sought after. Leaders are applauded. Leaders get things done; they make things happen. So, with all of this emphasis on leadership, we should be making progress, right? But ask yourself, is the world really becoming a better place to live?

THE NEED FOR LEADERSHIP

To find the answer, a person simply needs to look around. Our world is facing grave challenges and difficulties at every turn. Our homes, marriages, and social institutions are under attack. Instead of progressing, we seem to be falling behind at an ever-increasing rate. Why? We lack of true leadership. Yes, we have people in positions of leadership who have mastered the art of the sound bite. (Just tune in your daily news to observe "leaders" who are influential in the world's eyes, and yet something just isn't quite right on the inside.) A definite disconnect exists between the current emphasis on leadership and the actual leaders we are producing to take up crucial positions in government, in business, and in the family.

Even the church is facing the same challenges and experiencing the same shortage of true leaders. The divorce rate in Christian marriages continues to parallel the statistics of the general population at over fifty percent. Being associated with organized Christianity has become a liability in some ways because of the well-publicized moral failures of some church leaders.

We have embraced a Christianity that lifts up the name of Christ but is lacking the power of Christ. With the knowledge that something is missing, all too often we turn to the world for answers. Yet, instead of help, what we find is a culture swirling out of control—a place where Christ is marginalized or even vilified. The sad truth is that we are continually losing ground.

We also are confronted with our own limitations. We don't have enough strength, capacity, skills, or abilities in ourselves to meet the real needs we face or to accomplish all that we believe the Lord is calling us to do. Many leaders, whether in the marketplace or in the pastorate, are burning the candle at both ends, desperately trying to squeeze out just a little more of themselves and others to solve seeming insurmountable problems.

CONSIDER THE FOLLOWING STATISTICS:

- Every two seconds five people will die; four will be without Christ.[2]
- In the United States there is one trained Christian pastor for every 250 people. In the rest of the world, there is one trained Christian pastor for every 450,000 people.[3]

- In the next decade one billion people will come to Christ around the world. There is an overwhelming need to raise up and train millions of new pastors around the world in the next decade![4]
- Christian leaders around the world are predicting a leadership crisis in that there are not enough trained pastors and church planters in most parts of the world to deal with this great harvest.
- More than 2000 pastors are leaving the ministry in the USA each month. The dominant causes are burnout and moral failure.[5]
- Over 30 million children in the U.S. do not have a father living with them. This lack of fathers is the root of many negative societal issues.
  - » 90% of all homeless and runaway children are from fatherless homes.
  - » Over 71% of high school dropouts are from fatherless homes.
  - » Young children growing up without father's involvement are 10 times more likely to be poor.
  - » 63% of youths committing suicide come from fatherless homes.

BIGGER, BETTER, FASTER

I was sitting in a management team meeting listening to various heads of the organization (a ministry) talk about future goals when I heard something that just about knocked me out of my chair! But first, some background: As an organization, we were just coming out of a very challenging five-year rebuilding process. Due to lack of financial oversight and the overstepping of key leaders, the organization had been forced to reduce the head office staff by 70%. Finally, we were beginning to make some progress, and our current growth was moving in a positive direction—though still slow in comparison to similar organizations.

Okay, back to the meeting. Without prayer or consensus, the top leader declared that as a whole the organization was not performing well. His conclusion? "We need to do things BIGGER, BETTER, and FASTER!" He was visibly upset and obviously believed he had to push the team harder for greater results. Everyone—including me—was astounded. By his words and actions, this leader was saying that the "worth" of the organization came through its growth and impact. The people who comprised the ministry were being put down for not "producing."

You see, as a former businessman, this leader was trying to conduct spiritual work with worldly business skills. Unfortunately, this attitude is not isolated to this situation. It can be found in many, if not most, "Christian" organizations. Our minds are filled with thoughts like: "What are we doing for Jesus?" "We need to measure how much we are doing to determine whether or not we're successful." "We are doing better than our competitors, so we must be doing all right!" "If we don't show more results, our donors will jump ship and our funding will dry up." "Quick, do something—anything—and make it BIGGER, BETTER, and FASTER!"

> *"The Western world has been seduced by size. Size can justify almost anything. If a leader has grown an organization to a significant size, people take this as a sign of God's blessing. It may not necessarily be so. ... Bigger is not always better...the seduction is in believing that God is as impressed with crowds as people are. He is not!"*
> **Henry Blackaby**[6]

God reminds us that man's ways are not His ways: *"'For my thoughts are not your thoughts, neither are your ways my ways,' declares the Lord"* (**Isaiah 55:8 NIV**).

"We don't choose the times in which we live, whether good or bad, yet, we do choose how we spend the time given us, whether short or long."[7]

CHRISTIAN LEADERS ARE LOSING INFLUENCE

We are losing influence! As I teach and train leaders around this globe, I see secularism, materialism, and individualism on the rise. Our Western culture is struggling under the weight of potential financial collapse, tensions from other countries that despise us, and radical terrorists who want to kill us. A spiritual battle is raging, and we are struggling to hold on. The trend lines for many social issues like drug use, crime, and teenage pregnancy indicate control is slipping away. As the influence of the church declines, secular attitudes such as self-gratification are becoming central to our culture.

Just recently I was in Mexico, and I could see the fear and tension in the people's eyes and feel their hopelessness brought on by the daily threat of the drug wars. I met with a marketplace leader who lived on the Texas-Mexico border. He had just lost his brother, murdered by drug lords. Wickedness is filling the leadership void and holding people in bondage.

This erosion of influence is pervasive in all areas of our lives. The stakes are high and they are rising. What do we do? Where do we turn? Who are the leaders? Where are they? What is the solution?

> *"Where have all the leaders gone? They sometimes appear to be an endangered species, caught in a whirl of events and circumstances. But our quality of life depends on the quality of our leaders. As a person cannot function without a brain, so a society cannot function without leaders."*
> **Warren Bennis**[8]

HERE'S A NEWS FLASH: We don't need more programs, techniques, and methods to develop spiritually mature leaders! We don't need more leaders who are working hard out of their own set of resources. We don't need leaders doing more activity and starting new initiatives.

> **What we do need are true leaders—those leaders with access to resources beyond what they possess themselves.**

A survey of a thousand global Christian leaders at The Lausanne Global Conversation in 2010 summed it up well:

> *"We have a leadership problem! And it is a problem that must be solved in order for World Evangelization to flourish! If we look around us at the cry for Christ-centered leadership, it becomes clear that something is terribly wrong in our world."*

MY PERSONAL STORY

I have spent over 32 years working, coaching, and consulting in ministries to the marketplace along with 10 years at a large, multinational organization, Shell Oil Company. I have discovered that there are very few resources that address this leadership problem at its core. Much of what is offered focuses on leadership character, skills, and behavior rather than working from a different source entirely—Jesus Christ.

As a young man I held numerous leadership positions in college activities and in community endeavors. Being a self-starter, I took on as many responsibilities as I could in my secular job and in ministry. In just a few years I was one of the top sales executives for Shell and was being recognized nationally. My career and my life were doing quite well, and from the world's perspective I was very successful. My view was that the Lord and I made a good team—I would work hard and He would bless me.

When the Lord called me into vocational Christian work with Christian Business Men's Connection (CBMC), I thought I truly had something to offer, given my past success in the marketplace. In addition, I was very committed to expanding God's Kingdom. I had a feeling that joining up with the Lord was going to be a great thing. My wife and I relocated and plunged into ministry. We did not foresee, however, the rough waters that faced us.

Within days of the move, life began to turn upside down, and in a very short time the proverbial wheels came off the wagon. I was exhausted, frustrated, and struggling to make my spiritual life and my leadership work. It was then that I made the GREAT DISCOVERY:

> *God did not need me, yet He did want to use me. I was valued and loved for who I was in Christ. My security, significance, and acceptance were not based on my performance but on what Christ did for me.*

My struggle was not a punishment for wrongdoing (being a sinner). In fact, it demonstrated God's grace in that He wanted me to grow in my relationship with Him so that He could manifest His power through my weakness. This was both humbling and freeing. I was a saint in God's eyes who sometimes sinned.

The Christian life was much more about having an intimate relationship with Him and coming to know His life in me than it was trying harder to be like Jesus.

Over the last 22 years, I have been on a journey of discovery and growth—learning to allow Christ to live His life through me. In these years, I have applied these truths to my leadership roles, and God has done some amazing things. My spiritual life and leadership have been transformed.

I am totally committed to sharing these truths about Jesus Christ, the Leader, working through us. I have taught and trained thousands of leaders from some 50 countries. God is using this message to reproduce His Son in and

> *"The Christian Church has stagnated, largely due to its comfort with routines and rituals that are neither challenging nor relevant for millions of people. The Christian body is seeking leaders who will who will lead how Jesus led. There is a need for leaders who live and lead from a different starting point with a faith that is more vital and compelling."*
> **George Barna**

through these leaders, enabling them to engage in evangelism and discipleship with renewed power and a fresh sense of purpose.

SUMMARY

Our approach to developing leaders is not working well. The need is great. People are coming to Christ without a shepherd to guide and nurture them. Many broken homes and wayward young people are the direct result of leaderless families, businesses, and organizations. Individuals and organizations have put money and size ahead of God and godly values. Many churches and ministries look more like businesses and are run with a CEO mindset rather than a Christ-centered mindset.

Where are the leaders through whom God is working?

Go to LeadershipRevolution.us for additional resources on this topic and more.

ENDNOTES

1   Pollster on Christian and spiritual issues, http:www.barna.org
2   Source: Global Training Network
3   Source: East-West Ministries, Plano, TX
4   *Ministries Today* Magazine – May/June 2004 issue
5   Marble Retreat Center 2001
6   *Spiritual Leadership* by Henry Blackaby
7   Anonymous
8   Noted author on leadership whose books include *Managing People Is Like Herding Cats: Warren Bennis on Leadership* (1997) and *On Becoming a Leader* (1994)

Chapter Two

THE 10 MYTHS OF SPIRITUAL LEADERSHIP

". . . Apart from Me you can do nothing" (John 15:5).

SHIFTING THE PARADIGM

Fueling this leadership crisis are erroneous beliefs and assumptions, which form much of our current leadership paradigm. We will examine several of these faulty notions that believers have come to accept as "gospel" and will expose them for what they are: myths or, at best, half-truths. We will discover that these ideas have their foundation more in the world than they do in Christ and His Word. I want to empower you to shift your thinking about leadership to a new, more biblical paradigm—an altogether different way of leading.

A LEADERSHIP ASSESSMENT

How would you like to be a highly effective leader? Do you know what it takes to become a transformational leader? Would you like to increase your self-confidence, vision, wisdom, and impact? Do you want to be a person others turn to for direction?

Would you want to understand the leadership process for building a team whose members work together for positive outcomes? Do you long to experience the respect and personal growth that comes with effective leadership? In short, how satisfied are you with your current performance as a leader?

Everyone is a leader at some level, but biblical leadership doesn't just happen; it takes intentionality and a right perspective. It requires a willingness to learn and a deep commitment to growth.

Leadership development involves three primary aspects: (1) building and maintaining a solid foundation, (2) possessing and committing to a personal and relational growth process, and (3) equipping oneself with the necessary skills for increased leverage.

So where do we begin? It's hard to move forward if you don't know where you are. Leaders who expect to grow and become fruitful need to examine themselves and their work to see how they are doing.

By using the assessment tools that are included as part of this process, you will discover beliefs and perspectives about your leadership that need attention. Changes in your thinking will affect your actions and, ultimately, your results. This first assessment tool will help you to discover your current perspectives on leadership. Your answers will reveal opportunities for your growth.

Read each statement and circle "T" or "F" to indicate whether you believe it to be True or False. Then answer the two questions that follow.

To be an effective leader, you need more of Christ.	T	F
Growing leaders seek to feel closer to Jesus.	T	F
Fruitful leaders work hard for God.	T	F
The goal of a leader is to be like Jesus and lead like Jesus.	T	F
The leader's source of power comes from the spiritual disciplines.	T	F
Leadership begins with character as the foundation.	T	F
Leaders set the vision for their organization or team.	T	F
Leaders make things happen and show increasing results.	T	F
Leadership is first and foremost about influence.	T	F
If you are not in control, you will not be an effective leader.	T	F

Now, take some time to reflect on what makes a leader.

Based on the statements above, how are you doing?

What are the greatest challenges you face as a leader?

As you may have already guessed, the 10 statements in the assessment above are the 10 myths that I referred to at the beginning of this chapter! Surprised? I certainly was. Now, stick with me as we walk through each of them.

1. To be an effective leader, you need more of Christ.

When you come into a saving relationship with Jesus Christ, you receive the forgiveness of sins and eternal life. Your spiritual self goes from being dead to being fully alive. You don't receive *part* of the Spirit of Christ in this transaction; you receive the *fullness* of the Spirit.

As Christians and as spiritual leaders, we do not need more of Jesus Christ, because we already have all of Him in us. There is nothing more that we can be given. The truth is that we need to appropriate what we already have. The following verses indicate that we either have the Holy Spirit or we do not. There is no "half Spirit," just as an expectant mother cannot be "half pregnant."

"However, you are not in the flesh but in the Spirit, if indeed the Spirit of God dwells in you. But if anyone does not have the Spirit of Christ, he does not belong to Him. If Christ is in you, though the body is dead because of sin, yet the spirit is alive because of righteousness. But if the Spirit of Him who raised Jesus from the dead dwells in you, He who raised Christ Jesus from the dead will also give life to your mortal bodies through His Spirit who dwells in you" (**Romans 8:9-11**).

"And the testimony is this, that God has given us eternal life, and this life is in His Son. He who has the Son has the life; he who does not have the Son of God does not have the life" (**1 John 5:11-12**).

The primary problem is that too much of our *flesh*—our selfish nature—is blocking the release of the Spirit through us.

2. Growing leaders seek to feel closer to Jesus.

Often we say "I need to be closer to Christ," meaning that we do not "feel" close to Him. Yet that *feeling* does not truly reflect the *fact* of our relationship with Christ. Our feelings tend to arise from our emotions, which can give us a false reading of the status of our relationship. While these feelings may indicate that my *fellowship* with Christ needs improving, my *relationship* with Christ is forever secure and unchanging—I am loved unconditionally. There is nothing that will allow God to love me less or somehow to get God to love me more.

When we received Christ, we received Him into our spirit. He indwells us. We did not gain Someone who is merely walking alongside us, ahead of us, or behind us. He lives *in* us—we can't be any closer than that.

"The glory which You have given Me I have given to them, that they may be one, just as We are one; I in them and You in Me, that they may be perfected in unity, so that the world may know that You sent Me, and loved them, even as You have loved Me" (**John 17:22-23**).

"I have been crucified with Christ; and it is no longer I who live, but Christ lives in me; and the life which I now live in the flesh I live by faith in the Son of God, who loved me and gave Himself up for me" (**Galatians 2:20**).

3. **Fruitful leaders work hard for God and contribute to God's Kingdom work.**

Only God Himself working through us can accomplish His spiritual work. We cannot do anything that generates or contributes to God's spiritual work. We do not contribute anything of ourselves to the work of God. We simply participate in the work *He* is doing. God does not need us; He does not need our work done in our strength. *He wants to work through us to accomplish His plan and purpose.*

We live and lead *from* Him; we do not do things *for* Him.

Abide in Me, and I in you. As the branch cannot bear fruit of itself unless it abides in the vine, so neither can you unless you abide in Me. I am the vine, you are the branches; he who abides in Me and I in him, he bears much fruit, for apart from Me you can do nothing" (**John 15:4-5**).

We cannot do anything in God's Kingdom apart from Christ's accomplishing it through us as a result of an intimate relationship.

4. **The goal of a leader is to be like Jesus and lead like Jesus.**

As wonderful as this statement is, and even though it is very popular, the heart of it promotes self-effort and performance.

We will see that Jesus Himself led as a result of the relationship with His Father Who was abiding in Him—He did nothing on His own initiative.

*"Do you not believe that I am in the Father, and the Father is in Me? The words that I say to you **I do not speak on My own initiative,** but the Father abiding in Me does His works"* (**John 14:10, emphasis mine**).

The idea that Christ is our Life is in this verse, *"When Christ, who is our life, is revealed, then you also will be revealed with Him in glory"* (**Colossians 3:4**). Our spiritual life is derived from the life of Christ in us. As Paul wrote, *"for in Him we live and move and exist"* (**Acts 17:28**).

It boils down to this: Who is the source of power in your leadership—you or Christ? As a leader, is your focus on doing or being? When we say we want to be *like* Jesus, we are implying that *we* need to make this happen, rather than allowing the life of Christ to be expressed through us.

5. The leader's source of power comes from the spiritual disciplines.

There is an element of truth in this statement. Although the disciplines serve to help us grow and relate to Christ, it is His Spirit in us Who is the source of power. Consider this verse on where the source of power for every leader is found.

"And He has said to me, 'My grace is sufficient for you, for power is perfected in weakness.' Most gladly, therefore, I will rather boast about my weaknesses, so that the power of Christ may dwell in me. Therefore I am well content with weaknesses, with insults, with distresses, with persecutions, with difficulties, for Christ's sake; for when I am weak, then I am strong" (**2 Corinthians 12:9-10**).

We naively think that if we pray more and read the Word more, we will have more power. Not so. We have all of the power we need for the Spirit-filled life. Through His Word God enables us to exercise faith and appropriate the power of Christ that is already in us.

Don't get me wrong. The spiritual disciplines are absolutely critical to growing in the knowledge of Christ and becoming spiritually mature. The disciplines are the means to an end, which is an intimate relationship with Christ.

6. Leadership begins with character as the foundation.

Many Christian leaders have written that character is the foundation of leadership, such as this quote from Howard Hendricks, whom I respect very much: *"The crisis of leadership is a crisis of character."*[1]

Character is absolutely important to leadership because it is a cornerstone on which TRUST is built. Without character, there will be no leadership and we degenerate into selling, dictating, and organizing to make things happen. But, character has its foundation *in Christ*. Leadership begins with receiving Christ as Leader and living under His authority.

The Bible says that all authority has been given to Christ and that ultimately all authority is found in God the Father. *And Jesus came up and spoke to them, saying, 'All authority has been given to Me in heaven and on earth"* (**Matthew 28:18**). Leadership is the exercise of authority. We receive this authority when we receive Christ.

7. Leaders set the vision for their organization or team.

Leaders do not set the vision! Vision comes from God and God alone. Leaders cast vision that has been received from the Lord. Paul speaks of a vision he received from God: *"And a vision appeared to Paul in the night: a certain man of Macedonia was standing and appealing to him, and saying, 'Come over to Macedonia and help us.' And when he has seen the vision, immediately we sought to go into Macedonia, concluding that God had called us to preach the gospel to them"* (**Acts 16:9-10**).

> *"Many Christian leaders adopt the world's approach to vision and miss out on God's way. In seeking to serve the Lord, they inadvertently try to take on the responsibility of God. The truth is God is on mission to redeem humanity. He is the only one who knows how to do it. Leaders must understand, as Christ did, that their role is to seek the Father's will and adjust their life to Him. Too often Christian leaders operate under a false sense of assurance that they are seeking God's will. Being proactive by nature, leaders want to rush into action. As a result, they don't spend enough time seeking to hear clearly from God. . . . Asking God to set one's goals and to bless them doesn't ensure that they are from God. Only God can reveal his plans and does so in His way, on His schedule, and to whom He wills."*
>
> **Henry Blackaby**[2]

If God is the author of the vision, there will be unity and confirmation in the process. A vision from God will be clear, concise, and compelling.

8. Leaders make things happen and show increasing results.

This is a maxim from the world but not from the Word of God. As the One Leader, God is the source of results—He makes things happen. *"And we know that God causes all things to work together for good to those who love God, to those who are called according to His purpose"* (**Romans 8:28**).

God prepares us as clean, pure vessels in order to flow through us to produce results. God is at work beyond what we can see or think. He is solely in charge of the results, and leaders are simply stewards of the process.

9. Leadership is first and foremost about influence.

This statement is a classic half-truth. It is accurate, yet incomplete. Leadership is the role we play when Christ, the Leader in us, works through us to accomplish His will.

Influence comes from Christ's life in us as we follow Him and maintain an intimacy with Him. We are then prompted to live from our heart's passion to serve and value others. These qualities precede the influence. Without them, any influence will be diminished. We can see how influence grew as God worked through Paul.

"And the following day Paul went in with us to James, and all the elders were present. After he had greeted them, he began to relate one by one the things which God had done among the Gentiles through his ministry. And when they heard it they began glorifying God" (**Acts 21:18-20**).

10. If you not in control, you will not be an effective leader.

Every one of us, in our flesh, loves to be in control. Forfeiting control does not "feel good." The fact is, we have very little control over much of anything. For instance, we had no control over who our parents were, or when and where we were born. We had no control over the circumstances that shaped our upbringing.

However, we do have control over our attitudes, our value system, and how we spend our time. Effective leaders connect with God, yield control to Him, and trust Him with the results as they manage their stewardship responsibilities.

"Yours, O LORD, is the greatness and the power and the glory and the victory and the majesty, indeed everything that is in the heavens and the earth; Yours is the dominion, O LORD, and You exalt Yourself as head over all. Both riches and honor come from You, and You rule over all, and in Your hand is power and might; and it lies in Your hand to make great and to strengthen everyone" (**1 Chronicles 29:11-12**).

SUMMARY

I hope you can see that if we base our leadership on a set of myths or half-truths, we will not see God work in our daily lives as He extends His Kingdom. These half-truths lead to busyness, self-effort, division, infighting, and the splitting of organizations and churches.

We must embrace the fact that all truth has its origin in Christ and the Word as seen in **John 14:6**, *"I am the way, the truth, and the life"* and **John 17:17**, *"Sanctify them in truth, Thy word is truth."*

Leadership begins with our spiritual walk with Christ. That is our absolute top priority. Only when that is settled can we incorporate compatible principles found in the business world as an enhancement.

So are you ready to begin building a biblical framework of leadership that begins with the One Leader, Jesus Christ, and not yourself? Let's go!

Go to LeadershipRevolution.us for additional resources on this topic and more.

ENDNOTES

1   Howard G. Hendricks, noted Christian teacher and author (1924-2013)
2   *Spiritual Leadership* by Henry Blackaby

Chapter Three

AN ETERNAL LIFE LIVED IN A TEMPORAL WORLD

". . . Understand what the will of the Lord is" (Ephesians 5:17).

THE TEMPORAL AND THE ETERNAL

Recently I spoke at a CEO Forum on "Christ as the One Leader." The responses and questions I received were almost universal. "We have never thought of leadership in this way." "I will need to relearn much of what I have been taught on leadership." "Why does God allow people with poor character to get ahead?" "If I follow these principles will I succeed?" "How does this 'Christ as Leader' concept work?"

I believe we can find the answers as we ask a couple of other, more basic questions: How can we live spiritually in an everyday world? Asked in another way, how can leadership be lived out in the temporal and the eternal at the same time?

THE RISK OF LETTING GO

Ken Boa begins to address the tension between the eternal and the temporal in his book, *Conformed to His Image.*

> *Any attempt to pursue both the claims of the temporal and the eternal is like holding onto two horses that are galloping in opposite directions. The simultaneous pursuit of the kingdom of the world and the kingdom of Christ is impossible—at any*

point, one or the other will prevail. Many have tried to have it both ways, but this can never be more than a matter of adding a thin spiritual veneer over the same furniture that is manufactured and promoted by the world system.

It takes great risk to let loose of everything we have been taught to clamor after and control. It is never comfortable or natural to treasure the invisible over the visible, the promises of God over the promises of the world, the things that will not be fulfilled until the return of Christ over the things the world says we can have here and now. We want control and security on our own terms, yet the Scriptures tell us that the only true security comes from abandoning the illusion of control and surrendering ourselves unreservedly to the Person and purposes of God.[1]

LEADERSHIP AS AN ETERNAL LIFE

Leaders today most often begin with a view of obtaining certain outcomes, and to reach those goals, they emphasize principles relating to character, servant leadership, relational leadership, and team building. Now, because many of these principles are based on biblical truth, they bear fruit and certain desired outcomes are reached. Yet, almost all of this work can be done in the leader's own strength (operating in the flesh).

In contrast, true Christ Life Leadership begins with *Following*—an intimate, spiritual relationship with God Himself whereby His Spirit and His power are released through us. This intimacy is then reflected in our growing character, serving others, employing skills, and being Kingdom focused.

This truth has several implications:

1. The power released through the Life of Christ in us is infinite and ever-flowing. This is far beyond what we bring to the table in our limitations and experiences.

2. The challenge is that living this eternal life of leadership is no guarantee of success in the temporal world. In fact, we will be at war with the world, the flesh, and the devil. Obstacles will increase.

3. The ultimate reward or payout for Christ Life Leadership is in heaven, not in this life. Our life and leadership are reflective of our true hope.

CONFLICTING KINGDOMS?

Too often we buy in to the idea that the eternal and temporal are opposing kingdoms or, as Charles Colson described them, "Kingdoms in Conflict." The reality is that we have an eternal life that is lived on a temporal stage. We can't just live in one Kingdom; we must know and live with an integrated kingdom perspective. These two kingdoms exist together, and we function in them simultaneously. This does not mean, however, that these two kingdoms are equal in priority or in importance.

We live and work in a temporal world, all the while making choices and living from an eternal perspective and power. We are eternal beings working in a temporal setting, exercising specific roles and responsibilities by faith with an eternal hope. We are gloves, indwelt by an eternal Hand functioning for the good of others.

The challenge of this type of leadership is multifold:
1. Influence and character apart from Christ is nothing and *cannot* bear fruit. For the lost it is only a bigger ash heap, and for the carnal Christian it is wood, hay, and stubble.
2. The pursuit of the eternal (Christ, character, faith, and dependence) is not a guarantee for worldly success and "blessings."
3. Our true reward is in heaven. Secular work done with a spiritual motive is spiritual, and spiritual work done with a secular motive is secular.
4. We must learn to live in the "tension" of the eternal and the temporal.

5. We must realize, as the Psalmist did in Psalm 73, that evil people can and will get ahead for a time, maybe even a lifetime, yet in the end, when we are in the sanctuary, we will perceive their end.

We observe these truths about Christ Life Leadership.

1. It is a calling from the Lord to us. Leadership from Christ begins with our invitation to a relationship with Jesus (1 Corinthians 1:9). God desires this relationship more than we do and has provided everything necessary for it.

2. God's ways bear fruit. This fruit includes the "fruit of the Spirit" and the "fruit of new life." This leadership may not lead directly to more profit or better results. God has a much bigger and a much longer time horizon than we do. We live in His eternal world, and we cannot impose our temporal time frames or perspectives on God.

3. The goal of our leadership is to glorify God the Father and Jesus Christ. It is not to lift up ourselves or an organization. We practice this by becoming servants and helping others succeed.

4. This perspective and approach to leadership is a biblical alternative to teaching in the Christian community that emphasizes character, and teaching in the world that emphasizes influence.

5. Christ Life Leadership begins with Christ living in us by His Holy Spirit and being released through us to expand God's Kingdom.

6. The process embraces the idea of eternal reward as both a motivator and a governor for how we act.

7. The desired outcome is realized when the focus of leadership is on Kingdom impact.

HOW DO WE FUNCTION IN THIS LEADERSHIP CAPACITY?

We must first ask ourselves the following questions:

1. Who gets to define success?
2. What is success from God's perspective?
3. When will we receive our payout?

When we are left to ourselves and our desires, most of us want autonomy and independence. We desire to control and want to pursue our own ends. In this pursuit we often adopt the world's way of thinking and how it defines success. Our culture promotes the idea that this world is all there is. We then conclude, as a friend of mine said, "Get all you can, can all you get, and poison all the rest." The goals of life become the pursuit of pleasure and avoidance of pain.

Contrast that with the Christian perspective. We begin with the idea that God exists, He has our best interests at heart, and He is not playing a game of hide and seek. God has revealed Himself in the Bible, and it is in this book that true success is revealed.

When we embrace this view of God and how He works, it will affect the way we lead and motivate us to serve others.

DEFINING OUR VALUE SYSTEMS

Whether consciously or unconsciously, we all operate from a system of values—those ideals we hold to be most important and which guide our decision-making. Viewing ourselves as eternal beings living in a temporal world will shape these values toward God's purposes. If, on the other hand, we are not clear on the relative priority of these two worlds, the urgent and our desires for immediate gratification tend to win out.

A temporal value system is rooted in what the world defines as valuable and relies on our abilities and resources to gain it. It does not factor in God and dependence upon Him. An eternal value system in founded upon God and His character and is lived out "by faith" in Him. An eternal value system is based on what cannot be seen, yet it motivates us because of an eternal hope.

"For in hope we have been saved, but hope that is seen is not hope; for why does one also hope for what he sees? But if we hope for what we do not see, with perseverance we wait eagerly for it" (**Romans 8:24-25**).

We cannot have two worldviews or two value systems at the same time. We must define which will be our priority and thus will guide our activity in the world. Only with an eternal value system can we be grounded in our beliefs and not allow the world to define who we are by its sliding scale of importance based on fortune, fame, knowledge, looks, or performance.

God's plan and His value system based on it, is totally and fundamentally different than what the temporal world offers. We are to seek God over pleasure; we are called to serve people rather than to please or perform for people's approval; humility is valued over pride and position,

> *"Prosperity knits a man to the World. He feels that he is 'finding his place in it,' while really it is finding its place in him. His increasing reputation, his widening circle of acquaintances, his sense of importance, the growing pressure of absorbing and agreeable work, build up in him a sense of being really at home in earth."*
>
> **C. S. Lewis**[2]

and we are challenged to store up treasures in heaven rather than collect expensive trinkets on earth. To please God becomes our true pleasure, and He is the source of life. All else is a mere shadow.

A value system must be based on something with intrinsic worth or importance. Asking these questions can help us determine something's worth: "How long will the value of what I am seeking last?" "Will my possessions and rewards live on or fade away?" The Bible says that only two things will last—people and the Word of God; all else will deteriorate or burn up. This is why we are called to love and serve people, because by so doing we honor the Lord, we become conduits of Christ's love to them, they experience grace by our sacrifice, and we will be rewarded eternally. This kind of value system requires sacrifice and will cost us in the temporal, yet it will yield an infinite return in eternity.

Our value system will also reflect who we are and where we find security. Again, is my value as a person based on the "fickle finger of fate," or is it defined by a God who stands outside of time and declares me to be of infinite worth and value because He sent Jesus Christ to pay for my life?

Ken Boa describes this contrast of values systems:

TEMPORAL	ETERNAL
Pleasure	Knowing God
Recognition of People	Approval of God
Popularity	Servanthood
Wealth and Status	Integrity and Character
Power	Humility
↓	↓
Emptiness	Fulfillment
Delusion	Reality
Foolishness	Wisdom

"People think they want pleasure, recognition, popularity, status, and power, but the pursuit of these things leads, in the final analysis, to emptiness, delusion, and foolishness. God has set eternity in our hearts (Ecclesiastes 3:11), and our deepest desires are fulfillment (love, joy, peace), reality (that which does not fade away), and wisdom (skill in living). The only path to this true fulfillment lies in the conscious choice of God's value system over that which is offered by this world. This choice is based on trusting a Person we have not yet seen. 'And though you have not seen Him, you love Him, and though you do not see Him now, but believe in Him, you greatly rejoice with joy inexpressible and full of glory, obtaining as the outcome of your faith the salvation of your souls' (1 Peter 1:8-9)."[3]

So when we apply our value systems to our leadership roles and relationships, we must start with the Lord or else we will end up in the ditch faster than we can imagine.

The apostle Paul said, *"Therefore be careful how you walk, not as unwise men but as wise, making the most of your time, because the days are evil. So then do not be foolish, but understand what the will of the Lord is"* **(Ephesians 5:15-17).**

Let's make some practical application of these principles.

1. Consider if you had six months to live. What would you do? Who would you do it with? What would be your top priority?
2. Define what is your true hope. Hope is clarified in the times of the difficult to sustain when times are good. What do you hold as most important?
3. Set your value system.
4. Realize that life is short, so make it count with a clear life purpose statement.
5. Seek to make a difference daily in the lives of people by serving them.
6. Be thankful in all things—cultivate a heart of gratitude.

> *"The days of the years of our lives are few, and swifter than a weaver's shuttle. Life is a short and fevered rehearsal for a concert we cannot stay to give. Just when we appear to have attained some proficiency, we are forced to lay our instruments down. There is simply not time enough to think, to become, to perform what the constitution of our natures indicates we are capable of. ...How completely satisfying to turn from our limitations to a God who has none. Eternal years lie in His heart. For Him time does not pass, it remains; and those who are in Christ share with Him all the riches of limitless time and endless years."*
>
> A. W. Tozer[4]

BENEFITS OF AN ETERNAL LIFE OVER A TEMPORAL LIFE

When we possess a new nature and our spirit is indwelt by the Holy Spirit, we gain many benefits and advantages that are simply not possible for the non-believer.

The following are ten such blessings that we gain:

- **Security** – our security is in the unchanging Christ, not in the accolades of the world.
- **Significance** – our worth is based on the price God paid (Christ), not on our possessions or position.
- **Satisfaction** – our fulfillment is found in eternal things, not temporal.
- **Power** – our power comes from the infinite power of Christ rather than our limited resources.
- **Life** – we gain a life that lives on into eternity with God rather than hold on to a physical life that will end.
- **Wisdom** – God says He will give us His wisdom, which is far greater than our own.
- **Vision** – our vision comes from God, who is beyond time and space, rather than from our limited perspective.
- **Love** – we are loved unconditionally and forever by God, far better than the conditional love of people.
- **Wholeness** – an eternal life makes us whole; we are restored to function.
- **Peace** – God becomes our peace because we give up control and rest in Him.

A leader who does not have an eternal life (the Holy Spirit) does not possess any of these benefits and will futilely attempt to gain them from a world that is fickle and transitory.

This is the very reason why true leadership must begin with Christ rather than our character or our skills. Christ is the One who gives life to our character and skills.

LEADERSHIP IS A STEWARDSHIP

Managing God's Work

If we buy the idea that Christ is the One Leader and we are the vessel through whom God works, our leadership role changes from the owner of the outcome to the steward or manager of the process. This is the part we play. We don't add to or contribute to God's work—we participate in His work. We must function in our leadership with the right motives, with obedience, by valuing people, and serving with humility and excellence. In all of these activities we are seeking to honor and glorify God Himself. It is not about us, yet we have an absolutely vital role to play—steward. Paul, in **1 Corinthians 4:2,** says, *"Moreover it is required in stewards, that a man be found faithful"* (KJV). We are called to faithfulness.

We will examine three primary areas of our stewardship: (1) resources given by the Lord, (2) God's purposes, and (3) people. Before we unpack them, we must nail down the most challenging issue for a leader—*control*.

Giving Up Control

One of the hardest lessons for a leader to learn is to give up control and become a steward of the process. What does this mean? Let go and let God? Being passive? NEVER! It means that we seek God first and we listen to His direction. It means that we become neutral as to the outcome. We say to the Lord, "I am willing to go to the left or to the right, if You will make it clear." Our natural inclination is to let our fleshly patterns direct us to make things happen on our timetable and in our way. We want to achieve something great.

The more we seek to control our "worlds" by means of our efforts, the more we try to manipulate a particular outcome. By trying to hold on to this world and the things of it, we will resist the Lord and His ways. We will attempt to redefine the rules or sell our opinions in order to achieve our desires. Yet God is opposed to the proud and will give grace to the humble.

Stewarding the process includes listening to God, being obedient, working with excellence, and valuing people in our decisions. Consider these thoughts from my friend Tom Atema, who has literally trained thousands of leaders worldwide:

> *"We must have the skills to develop people, communicate, build teams, and solve problems; however, building your skills is not the number one priority. Strategic formation, the 'know-how' to be an effective planner, set priorities, cast vision, and develop other leaders, is another possible choice for number one – but...! Yep, not number one either.*
>
> *"I believe the number one 'skill,' if you can call it that, is the skill to be open to the voice of God. I think it is a lost skill for leaders today. In fact, the longer I lead and the longer I am on this leadership journey, the more convinced I am that the majority of my leadership is not driven by my character, skill, or strategic thinking. It has far more to do with my skill—my ability—and willingness—to be open to the "still, small voice" of the Lord. Actually, this voice is not small at all, but powerful—more powerful than the other skills I mentioned. I think it is a skill because we have to learn to stay open, learn the habit of willingness, to have the constant ability to hear the voice of the Lord. Today, we tend to place so much time on developing our skills, developing a strong character, or developing our strategic plans that we fail to hear His voice.*
>
> *"We must never lose the skill of listening to the voice of God. This skill develops over time and with much practice. When we do not listen to the voice of God in our lives as leaders, the results can be devastating. Often it takes weeks, even years to recover from the mess created or the opportunities missed by not listening and acting on that still, small voice of our Lord in us. Sometimes, we never recover."[5]*

A Steward of Resources

As we learn to give up control and allow God to take the reins, there is still plenty for us to do. As has been said, it is not a "Let go and let God" philosophy, which can only produce passivity and presumption. Our role is to oversee the use of the resources God has provided, both individually and to the work. The personal resources are our eternal life, time, talent, and treasure. The resources of the work begin with the vision that God provides.

Christ's Resources Are Our Resources

"Just as Jesus knew who He was, where He came from, and where He was going, so all who have put their trust and hope in Him should know the same. But few do. It is only as we frequently renew our minds with the spiritual truth of the Scriptures that we will move our thinking into alignment with the reality of who we are in Christ. Like Christ, we have dignity and power; every spiritual blessing has been given into our hands (Ephesians 1:3, 19; 3:16, 20-21). We also have significance and identity; we have become the children of God (Romans 8:16; 1 John 3:1-2). And we have been given the security and destiny of knowing that nothing can separate us from the love of God in Christ (Romans 8:18, 35-39). These limitless resources meet our deepest needs and overcome the human dilemma of loneliness, insignificance, and meaninglessness.

"When these truths begin to define our self-image, they make us secure enough to love and serve others without seeking our own interests first. Because of our security and significance in Christ, we do not need to be controlled by the opinions and responses of others. We have nothing to prove because we know who and whose we are. Rather than trying to impress and manipulate people, we can do our work with excellence

as unto the Lord (Colossians 3:23). The more we are concerned with what God thinks of us, the less we will be worried about what others think of us. And when we are no longer enslaved to people's opinions of us, we are free to love and serve them as Christ loves us—with no strings attached."[6]

God has given each of us varying amounts of time, talent, and treasure. Our role is to utilize well the gifts we have been given rather than becoming caught up in comparison, envy, or gaining from others. We each must walk in dependence on the Lord for how we use the resources He has given to us, and in the end we must each give an account for how well we used them.

A Steward of God's Purposes

God placed us here on earth as His instruments to carry out His purposes. We are His hands and feet. He can and desires to operate through us to accomplish His work. We are not to be focused on our purposes and desires primarily. We are to align ourselves with God and fit into His bigger plan.

Thus the end of our activities and goals should be to please the Lord and be used to extend His Kingdom. Thus, we are to always be engaged in evangelism and discipleship in all aspects of our life. "Go and make disciples" is a command, and we will be held accountable or rewarded to the degree that we obey.

A Steward of People

By definition, leaders always work with people—we are to *lead* and *manage* them. It is not an either/or proposition. We give guidance and direction to empower people to participate in an endeavor. We manage their collective assets (the pool of gifts, talents, personalities, knowledge), and we put the right people in the right places at the right time in order for them to do their best.

As leaders, we must know each person and what they bring to the table, and with that knowledge we can help them grow and fully participate in the work of the team.

How Does a Leader Exercise Stewardship?

"Steward" is both a role and an attitude. The following list will give you some action steps in making your stewardship practical and alive. Consider **Luke 16:10-11**, *"He who is faithful in a very little thing is faithful also in much; and he who is unrighteous in a very little thing is unrighteous also in much. Therefore if you have not been faithful in the use of unrighteous wealth, who will entrust the true riches to you?"*

- **Faithful** – we are called to be faithful stewards, which means "full of faith" and "to be diligent or trustworthy."
- **Thankful in all things** – we must be grateful for the good and the difficult. Gratitude helps us lead and manage well, in addition setting a positive atmosphere.
- **Give Credit** – great leaders lift up the people and don't take credit for the team's accomplishments; they reflect it back to others and ultimately to the Lord.
- **Work with Excellence** – leaders do things very well. This sets a right model to follow and will help the team accomplish the goals.
- **Right Motives** – we need to do things for the right reasons and in the right way. God does not work on the premise that the end justifies the means.

Stewards of the Manifold Grace of God

A final aspect of leaders as stewards involves their handling of God's grace, *"As each one has received a special gift, employ it in serving one another as good stewards of the manifold grace of God. Whoever speaks, is to do so as one who is speaking the utterances of God; whoever serves is to do so as one who is serving by the strength which God supplies; so that in all things God may be glorified through Jesus Christ, to whom belongs the glory and dominion forever and ever. Amen"* (**1 Peter 4:10-11**).

Simply put, this grace of God is a special gift given to every believer, and all of our actions and attitudes need always to reflect Jesus Christ as we serve one another! The strength and courage to do so comes from God alone.

PARADOX OF THE CHRISTIAN LIFE AND SPIRITUAL LEADERSHIP

A paradox is a statement that doesn't seem to make sense at first but, when properly understood, makes a lot of sense. The Christian life and Spiritual leadership are two paradoxes that Jesus taught and modeled.

- **We find by losing** – *"He that finds his life shall lose it, and he that loses his life for my sake shall find it"* (**Matthew 10:39**).
- **We receive by giving** – *"Give, and it shall be given unto you; good measure, pressed down, and shaken together, and running over, shall men give into your bosom. For the measure you give will be the measure you get back"* (**Luke 6:38**).
- **We are exalted by being humble** – *"Whoever exalts himself will be humbled, and whoever humbles himself will be exalted"* (**Matthew 23:12**).
- **We become great by becoming small** – *"Whoever humbles himself like this child, he is the greatest in the kingdom of heaven"* (**Matthew 18:4**).
- **Our weakness is our strength** – "And he said unto me, *"My grace is sufficient for you, for my power is made perfect in weakness. I will all the more gladly boast of my weaknesses, that the power of Christ may rest upon me. For the sake of Christ, then, I am content with weaknesses, insults, hardships, persecutions, and calamities; for when I am weak, then I am strong"* (**2 Corinthians 12:9-10**).
- **We lead by serving** – *"You know that those who are supposed to rule over the nations lord it over them, and their great men exercise authority over them. But it shall not be so among you; but whoever would be great among you must be your servant, and whoever would be first among you must be slave of all"* (**Mark 10:42-45**).

- **We live by dying** – *"I am crucified with Christ; nevertheless I live; yet not I, but Christ lives in me; and the life which I now live in the flesh I live by faith of the Son of God, who loved me, and gave himself for me"* **(Galatians 2:20)**.

If the Christian life is a series of paradoxes, then the actions of individual Christians should make non-Christians wonder what makes them "tick." The very fact that Christians live and act in ways opposite of non-Christians should challenge their whole approach to life! The same should be true for Christians in everyday leadership roles!

ONE LEADER PRINCIPLE: As a leader, our fundamental role is to be a steward of God's life, purposes, and work while He flows through us to produce His outcome.

ONE LEADER PRAYER: (personalize this passage as a prayer to God)

"As each one has received a special gift, employ it in serving one another as good stewards of the manifold grace of God. Whoever speaks, is to do so as one who is speaking the utterances of God; whoever serves is to do so as one who is serving by the strength which God supplies; so that in all things God may be glorified through Jesus Christ, to whom belongs the glory and dominion forever and ever. Amen" **(1 Peter 4:10-12)**.

ENDNOTES

1   *Conformed to His Image* by Ken Boa, Zondervan (2001)
2   *The Screwtape Letters* by C. S. Lewis
3   Op. Cit., Boa
4   *The Knowledge of the Holy*, A. W. Tozer
5   Tom Atema, VP of EQUIP International Ministries and Strategic Partnerships
6   Op. Cit, Boa

Chapter Four

THE ONE LEADER MODEL – A NEW LEADERSHIP PARADIGM

"He [Jesus] has a right to interrupt your life. He is Lord. When you accepted Him as Lord, you gave Him the right to help Himself to your life anytime He want. We may want to do something FOR God and God says DON'T try. The more significant thing is to see what God wants to do in and through people."

Henry Blackaby[1]

"I remember an early lesson taught when I was a little leaguer. It was as simple as it was elemental to the game: if you want to catch the ball, you've got to open your baseball glove. Take the posture of receptivity. Open your hands, your heart and your mind that you may receive from God what you most need."

Dr. Steve Wilson, Oakmont
Presbyterian Church

"If you leave the church service thinking about how good the pastor was, he has missed the mark. If you leave consumed with Christ, the pastor has been used by the Lord."

Howard Hendricks[2]

LEADERSHIP IS RECEIVED NOT ACHIEVED

If Christ is the One Leader, we fulfill the role of leadership in the arena of influence where He has placed us. Life, power, wisdom, and vision that are necessary to fulfill your leadership responsibilities are all received from Christ.

Because we have received the Spirit of Christ in us, we received Him as the One Leader in us. As we have seen in the previous chapter, the world's approach to leadership is to seek an objective that can be achieved in our strength. This is not so in the spiritual arena. The following illustration can help us grasp how this works in everyday life.

THE HAND IN THE GLOVE

Can a glove do anything by itself? Absolutely NOT! Gloves participate in the activity of the hand. They play only a role or function. They are not a source of power. Every glove is designed and made with its end use in mind. A surgical glove is thin, soft, supple, and able to conform to every movement of the hand, however slight. It is sterile in order to provide protection to both the patient and the surgeon. It works well because it is made that way and is empowered solely by the hand of the user.

What does this look like in our lives? When faced with a decision or a choice between two directions, we must seek the Lord's guidance through prayer, the Word, counsel, and circumstances. We should seek wisdom and direction from above before we attempt to reach our personal goals.

Recently when I was faced with a vocational change, it was a time of transition with no clear-cut solutions. I was moving out of an organization and I had three options: (1) start a ministry, (2) seek a role with an established ministry, or (3) go back into business. The business option was especially attractive—the money, security, and upside growth were remarkable. To go with another organization offered benefits and a level of stability. The start-up ministry choice was the most uncertain and risky, but probably the most focused on God's Kingdom work.

The counsel I received was varied and, in fact, supported all three options. My wife knew my heart and passion, and she encouraged me to follow my passion in spite of its being the least certain. As I studied the Bible and prayed, there came an overwhelming sense of peace and an inner compelling for me to start a ministry focused on Christ as the One Leader. He answered prayers and gave me specific promises from the Bible. It has now been over three years since this new work began, and ministry is taking place on five continents. I was available to hear from God and follow His leading and His leadership as He opened doors of opportunity. He has worked in unusual ways and displayed power that can only be explained by His supernatural work.

In practice, becoming the glove means being available, trusting in God's wisdom and direction, and giving up control of the ultimate out- comes. It's the giving up of control, either perceived or real, that is most difficult!

JESUS' MODEL OF LEADERSHIP

Jesus modeled leadership throughout His ministry. One of the most defining moments was the night before His crucifixion. As He taught the disciples in the upper room, He took a towel and began washing His disci- ples' feet. In that moment, we see the following process emerge: Jesus was willing to humble Himself and *follow* the Father based on a relationship. He *served* the disciples by taking up the towel, and He *influenced* them by challenging them to go and do likewise.

After washing the disciples' feet, Christ used the metaphor of the vine, the branches, and the fruit: *"Abide in Me, and I in you. As the branch cannot bear fruit of itself unless it abides in the vine, so neither can you unless you abide in Me. I am the vine and you are the branches, he who abides in Me and I in him, he bears much fruit, for apart from Me you can do nothing"* **(John 15:4-5).**

From this picture of the vine, branch, and fruit we see three overarch- ing aspects of leadership:

1. **The vine** – Jesus Christ, and He is the source of life and nutrients for the branch and the producer of the fruit. The vine connects to the branch.

2. **The branch** – the believers who are grafted into the vine, and it is the conduit between the vine and the fruit. Branches grow in all directions and are the fruit-bearers.
3. **The fruit** – new life (new believers, spiritual growth, etc.) It is the product of the vine and food for others.

The essence of the vine (Christ) is **SPIRITUAL**; the branch pictures who we are and what role we perform, which is **RELATIONAL**; the outcome of the spiritual working through the relational is the fruit, which is **MISSIONAL**. These three primary characteristics form the framework for the seven Christ Life Leadership Principles.

7 CHRIST LIFE LEADERSHIP PRINCIPLES

Spiritual
1. There is One Leader and You are … Not It!
2. Leadership is released through Brokenness and Surrender.

Relational
3. Leadership is formed by Following First.
4. Leadership is modeled by Serving as Second.
5. Leadership is expanded by Influencing to the Third and Fourth Generations.

Missional
6. Leadership is leveraged through Teamwork.
7. Leadership is focused on God's Kingdom and leaves a Lasting Legacy.

CHRIST LIFE LEADERSHIP REQUIRES GRACE

Christ Life Leadership is built on and requires grace. This grace does not come from us but from Christ and His sacrifice on the cross. It is important to capture the essence and the cost of this grace.

Dietrich Bonhoeffer argued that as Christianity spread, the Church became more "secularized," accommodating the demands of obedience to Jesus to the requirements of society. In this way, "the world was Christianized, and grace became its common property." But the hazard of this was that the gospel was cheapened, and obedience to the living Christ was gradually lost beneath formula and ritual, so that in the end, grace could literally be sold for monetary gain.

> *"Cheap grace is the preaching of forgiveness without requiring repentance, baptism without church discipline. Communion without confession. Cheap grace is grace without discipleship, grace without the cross, grace without Jesus Christ."*

The main defect of such a proclamation is that cheap grace contains no demand for discipleship. In contrast to this is costly grace:

> *"Costly grace confronts us as a gracious call to follow Jesus, it comes as a word of forgiveness to the broken spirit and the contrite heart. It is costly because it compels a man to submit to the yoke of Christ and follow him; it is grace because Jesus says: 'My yoke is easy and my burden is light.'*

> *"Costly grace is the treasure hidden in the field; for the sake of it a man will gladly go and sell all that he has. It is the pearl of great price to buy which the merchant will sell all his goods. It is the kingly rule of Christ, for whose sake of one will pluck out the eye which causes him to stumble; it is the call of Jesus Christ at which the disciple leaves his nets and follows him. ...*

> *"It is costly because it condemns sin, and grace because it justifies the sinner. Above all, it is costly because it cost God the life of his Son: 'ye were bought at a price,' and what has cost God much cannot be cheap for us. Above all, it is grace because God did not reckon his Son too dear a price to pay for our life, but delivered him up for us."*[3]

TWO TYPES OF LEADERSHIP

In a similar fashion, we have taken what the Bible says about Jesus Christ as a leader and refashioned leadership into our image and likeness. In our current Christian world we made have popular the phrase, "Leadership is influence, nothing more, nothing less." We have made leadership equivalent to "results" and "making things happen." To achieve this end, the focus becomes the outward behavior, the charisma, the skills and talents of the person in charge. This has been promoted globally as the method for being more effective in God's work. Like "cheap grace" was the deadly enemy of the church, this "leadership is influence" is the deadly enemy of God's Kingdom work because it begins with us and looks at outcomes as if we contributed to God's work.

We have cheapened the role of our true Leader, Jesus Christ, by producing a formula or process for how we can lead for Jesus. Christ has been taken out of equation; we are now central, and the results rest on our abilities and aptitudes. One lifts up man, while the other lifts up Christ. This is a primary reason why the church is impotent and the enemy is winning the battles. Our victory and influence will only come as we establish Jesus Christ as Leader in our hearts.

Note the difference between these two types of leadership:

LEADERSHIP IS INFLUENCE	CHRIST AS LEADER
Our best effort and hard work	Our surrender and His work
Outward skills	Inward Spirit
Rely on talents	Requires faith
Human and/or worldly power	Supernatural power
Being in control	Following God's Call
Begins with the mind	Starts with the heart
Teaches behavior	Teaches brokenness

Establishing Christ as the One Leader in your heart will be costly, it will require a total surrender, a giving up of your best efforts done in your strength. Christ will be glorified rather than shining the spotlight on a man, an organization, or a method.

You undoubtedly have heard the line, *"If you have no followers, you are only taking a walk."* This makes great copy, yet it shifts the focus to ourselves and our work. Christ is the Leader and as we follow Him, His leadership flows through us.

Christ as Leader is costly because it requires you to follow Him and serve others, putting them ahead of yourself. It will cost in this lifetime because others may take the credit and all you have invested may be pushed to the side of the road. People will not understand, and they will implore you to be more "like" Jesus. Living as Paul taught "for me to live is Christ and die is gain" is more than simply doing what Jesus would do.

It will cost you in donations and funding for your work because you just don't have the big headlines or results. Heaven's work is more in the heart than in the streets. Not to worry, for God knows your heart and He knows the work He has done through you.

Christ as the One Leader connects and embraces this costly grace because it is about a life in a life. Bonhoeffer comments,

> *"Such grace is costly because it calls us to follow, and it is grace because it calls us to follow Jesus Christ. It is costly because it costs a man his life, and it is grace because it gives a man the only true life."*[4]

LEADERSHIP IS MORE THAN INFLUENCE

This first diagram starts on the right-hand side with the world's typical view: "leadership is influence." If this is our starting point of leadership, then the foundation and character are often overlooked or missed altogether. The results become all-important as we adopt a belief that the end justifies the means. We need to shift the paradigm of leadership by moving two steps back before we move forward.

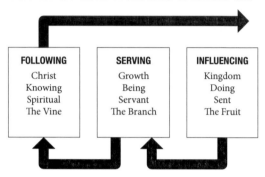

Thus the illustration shows arrows moving back from influencing to serving and then to following. It is only from this place of following that we develop a spiritual foundation, display a servant's heart, and bring an inspiring influence to bear fruit in God's Kingdom.

THE LEADERSHIP GROWTH PROCESS

The second illustration looks at the growth process. True leadership growth is an inside-out process. Here we use three concentric circles. The center begins with "Following," which is *knowing* Christ. To grow we move outward to "Serving," which begins with *being*—who we are as a leader. Finally we move to "Influenc-

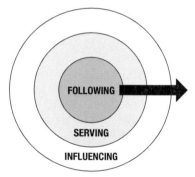

ing" as we engage in God's Kingdom through our *doing*. Lasting change does not occur from the outside in. We must first address our relationship with God, which in turn allows us to shape our relationships, which will affect our actions and behavior.

WORLDVIEW, VALUES, AND BEHAVIOR

In this diagram, we can also equate these three concentric circles to worldview, values, and behavior. At the core is our worldview, which is our perspective about life and God. This is framed by our spiritual man being filled with the Spirit of Christ. This is our relationship with God and Christ known as "Following" and has as its foundation three components (identity, indwelling, and intimacy). This worldview represents the truths upon which our faith rests and takes action.

> **"Christianity is a way of seeing and comprehending all reality. It is a worldview."**
> **Charles Colson**

This worldview shapes our values which is the next ring or circle. Our values are what we hold to be most important. Our values are made up of Character (personal choices), Community (relationships), and Calling (vocation and purpose). Our worldview shapes our values, which in turn affect our behavior. Our behavior is characterized by actions and laboring in God's Kingdom purposes.

BALANCE IS NOT THE ANSWER

Recently a young man was sharing with me his frustration of attempting to grow spiritually and be fruitful in his walk with Lord, to be God's man in the marketplace, and to deepen his relationship with a young girl. "I see my selfishness and prideful attitudes. I am struggling! I try to spend time with the Lord, and I pack my schedule extremely full to be as productive as possible. I am out of balance. How do I get back to being balanced?"

I shared with him that being out of balance is a good diagnostic tool— we almost always can recognize when things are spinning out of control and our gyroscope begins to wobble. Yet the answer is not balance! Trying to achieve balance is usually us seeking to maintain control. We double down and do more of the right things (spiritual disciplines) and less of the bad (flesh, pride, etc.). This may provide temporary relief, yet it will never get us back to balance. Balance is the overflow of an integrated life.

If balance were the solution, we would invariably compartmentalize our life and put Christ in a box, our work in a box, our relationships in a box, and so on. There will never be enough time or margin to achieve success with this approach. Life and real balance are not about doing more.

Only when Christ is our life and He is integrated into every one of our daily activities will we sense balance.

Christ as life is experienced when we receive His love and affection and don't try to achieve this intimate relationship by adding more disciplines or doing more ministry. We know our identity is found in Christ alone and not in our accomplishments or our image. His indwelling life is the source of our spiritual life, wisdom, and power.

If our leadership is going to be effective and fruitful, it must flow from Christ into Following, Serving, and Influencing. They all are vitally important. When we begin our growth process, any one of the three may be our strength. In the end we must seek to grow in all three components.

In summary, we must keep in mind the following:

- All three leadership components are of equal importance.
- Your leadership will not stand on one or two components.
- The three components work together to bear fruit.

THE ONE LEADER MODEL

The **One Leader Model** reflects the unlimited spiritual resources of Jesus Christ with which the Holy Spirit leads others through us. Rather than focusing on outcomes alone, this leadership model is a three-fold development process.

We see this trilogy in many ways, as the following chart shows. The beauty of this model is that it encompasses many aspects of leadership that are taught and puts them into a comprehensive approach rather than focusing or emphasizing one aspect over another.

FOUNDATION		PROCESS		FOCUS
Christ	>	Leader	>	Eternal Kingdom
Spiritual	>	Relational	>	Missional
Spirit	>	Soul	>	Body
Worldview	>	Values	>	Behavior
God	>	Others	>	World
From	>	Through	>	To
Intimacy	>	Community	>	Ministry
Knowing	>	Being	>	Doing
Upward	>	Inward	>	Outward
Power	>	Emptiness	>	Results
Beginning	>	Middle	>	End
Launch	>	Journey	>	Destination
FOLLOWING		**SERVING**		**INFLUENCING**

Each component begins with a spiritual foundation, moves to a leadership process, and ends with an eternal focus. Again, the development process for a leader is:

- Following First
- Serving as Second
- Influencing to the Third and Fourth Generations.

Let's examine what the Bible says about the **Following-Serving-Influencing** process model for leaders and their spiritual growth.

FOLLOWING FIRST

Jesus did not focus on doing great things; He concentrated on being aligned with the Father and fulfilling His will. He followed as the Father directed. Leadership does not begin with leading but following!

When Jesus called His disciples to Himself, He didn't say, "Come and be a leader! Join my team and change the world!" Christ was intentional by challenging the disciples to "follow" Him. Consider the following verses.

"Then Jesus said to His disciples, 'If anyone wishes to come after Me, he must deny himself, and take up his cross and follow Me. For whoever wishes to save his life will lose it; but whoever loses his life for My sake will find it'" (**Matthew 16:24-25**).

Jesus called His disciples "to follow" on many occasions. "To follow" means to abandon a current course or direction and to go after Christ. It combines giving up and receiving. For the disciples, this "following" involved sacrifice and was motivated out of Christ's love for them and the their love for Christ.

"And He said to them, 'Follow Me, and I will make you fishers of men.' Immediately they left their nets and followed Him" (**Matthew 4:19-20**).

"Then Jesus again spoke to them, saying, 'I am the Light of the world; he who follows Me will not walk in the darkness, but will have the Light of life'" (**John 8:12**).

PRINCIPLE: *Leaders must follow first. They must develop an abiding love relationship that submits to and obeys the Lord before they gain the spiritual capacity for others to follow them.*

SERVING AS SECOND

To be a "serving" leader, our focus is not on ourselves but on others. God and others are first; we are second. We are helping, encouraging, and building up people from our spiritual relationship with the Father. As such, we are giving away something God has given us. He is flowing His Spirit, love, and power "through" us for the benefit of others.

The "through" of leadership paints the picture that although we participate in the process of leading, the power, life, and wisdom come from Jesus who then is working through us. We are conduits or vessels while He is the source. Although the Lord could achieve what He wants with or without us, He chooses to work through us as His ambassadors to accomplish His Kingdom purposes. Examine these verses and see how God works "through" a person to perform His will.

"When they had arrived and gathered the church together, they began to report all things that God had done with them and how He had opened a door of faith to the Gentiles" (**Acts 14:27**).

"When they arrived at Jerusalem, they were received by the church and the apostles and the elders, and they reported all that God had done with them" (**Acts 15:4**).

"God was performing extraordinary miracles by the hands of Paul" (**Acts 19:11**).

Paul acknowledged on these numerous occasions that God did His OWN work "through" human hands and feet. Paul did not take credit for it or attempt to have the world shine its light on him.

Serving Was the Essence of Jesus' Leadership on Earth

Serving is leadership in action. The idea of servant leadership has been around since the time that the Bible was written. We see leaders who used their position and power for the greater good of those around them. Jesus was our prime example of being a servant, especially on the night before going to the cross.

Jesus was responding to a debate among the disciples about who was the greatest in Luke 22:24-30. His actions reinforced His teaching. He said he did not come to be served but to serve, and then took up a towel and began to wash the disciples' feet. The disciples were shocked.

"And there arose also a dispute among them as to which one of them was regarded to be greatest. And He said to them, "The kings of the Gentiles lord it over them; and those who have authority over them are called 'Benefactors.' But it is not this way with you, but the one who is the greatest among you must become like the youngest, and the leader like the servant. For who is greater, the one who reclines at the table or the one who serves? Is it not the one who reclines at the table? But I am among you as the one who serves" (**Luke 22:24-27**).

"For the Son of man did not come to be served, but to serve and give Himself a ransom for many" (**Mark 10:45**).

"The evening meal was being served.... Jesus knew that the Father had

put all things under his power, and that he had come from God and was returning to God; so he got up from the meal, took off his outer clothing, and wrapped a towel around his waist. After that, he poured water into a basin and began to wash his disciples' feet, drying them with the towel that was wrapped around him" (**John 13:2-5**).

When we serve people who do not expect it, they will take notice. Yet what stops this from happening? Picture this in your mind: We as leaders are conduits, and God is the fluid. The size of the pipe and the force of the fluid will determine how much comes out at the end. We cannot control the force of the fluid. We can control whether we as pipes have any obstructions (sin issues). Are you a clean pipe? We also realize that as the pipe expands more fluid is able to flow through it. The expansion of the pipe is a picture of growing and maturing. How is the Lord maturing and growing you?

We do not add to what God does, yet we can restrict His work through us.

INFLUENCING TO THE THIRD AND FOURTH GENERATIONS

Influencing is a process of engaging in God's mission to reach the world by equipping leaders to catalyze movements of evangelism and discipleship. In this process the Lord uses each of our unique gifts, talents, and skills to influence others. We are called to work together in the body of Christ and in teams because no one has all of the gifts. We need one another. This leadership of influence is directed towards the Kingdom work of God. This modeling of influence is found in Paul's life: *"Brethren, join in following my example, and observe those who walk according to the pattern you have in us"* (**Philippians 3:17**). We see the influencing of the next generations as he prepares Timothy: *"The things which you have heard from me in the presence of many witnesses, entrust these to faithful men who will be able to teach others also"* (**2 Timothy 2:2**). Note the four generations: Paul, Timothy, faithful men, and others also.

God is always working and leading, sometimes in spite of us. We realize that He is never late in any and all things that He is doing. He is at work, and we need to wake up and recognize it. We are called to engage and participate with Him in His work as Paul did: *"All the people kept silent, and they were listening to Barnabas and Paul as they were relating what signs and wonders God had done through them among the Gentiles"* (**Acts 5:12**).

It is fundamentally important to realize the following:

PRINCIPLE: *God is not interested in our work for Him; He is only focused on His work through us.*

We want to be clear that our leadership role is a gift we have received, and our capacity (eternal life, power, wisdom, vision) as a leader is also a gift that must be received and put to use.

We receive leadership as a gift through which we exercise faithful stewardship of the precious treasures given to us, resulting in influence.

Leadership Application

The practical application of the Follow-Serve-Influence model of leadership comes down to how a leader handles the issues of control and results.

We all want to be in control. Many of us act like we are in control. We desire certain outcomes and work hard to achieve them. We think we can handle any task that comes before us. The challenge comes when we are faced with situations or circumstances that are beyond our capacity. Then our tendency is to take matters into our hands, and often that entails manipulation, grabbing, or running over others in order to get the results we want. These actions are not an evidence of spiritual leadership but a demonstration of selfishness. Our thinking is that the end justifies the means.

Furthermore, desiring to control leads is to compete, compare, and count in order to gain a measure of stature or identity. To *compete* is to "strive to outdo another for acknowledgment, a prize, supremacy, profit, or using people for gain." To *compare* is to "examine in order to highlight similarities and differences for discovery or for personal gain." To *count* is to "add one by one to determine the total number." All three of these are attempts to be the center of attention.

If I am in control, it follows that I will have my own self-interests at heart. On the surface, this sounds good, yet it only leads to "self" being central as in self-preservation, self-protection, self-absorption, or a multiple of other self-centered behaviors. These behaviors are not other-centered and do not lead to servant leadership.

If God is in control, I must embrace the idea that He also controls the content, the flow, and the timing of all things in my life. The implications of this are staggering and can only be accepted by faith. If I believe that God is in control, I must also believe that He has my best interests at heart. He loves me unconditionally. God allows the good, the bad, and the ugly into my life for my good. If, as a leader, I can embrace the fact that God is in control and that He has my best interests at heart, then I can find contentment in any circumstance.

When we surrender to Christ as Lord, we become servants and stewards of the process. We do *our best* with all excellence rather than focusing on being *the best*. This is a place of rest that comes from exercising dependence and faith in the character and nature of God, producing contentment.

Paul said, *"I have learned to be content in whatever circumstances I am. I know how to get along with humble means, and I also know how to live in prosperity; in any and every circumstance I have learned the secret of being filled and going hungry, of having abundance and suffering need"* (Philippians 4:11-12).

LEADER "SHIFT"

In applying this new paradigm of leadership, we must "shift" from old ways of thinking to a new way leading. In fact, many of the old ways are simply the world's way with a different color of paint.

Each of the seven principles requires overcoming a temptation or sin by shifting the paradigm or practice to put Christ and His work at the center of your leadership.

LEADERSHIP PRINCIPLE	TEMPTATION OR SIN	"SHIFT"	EXAMPLE	SCRIPTURE
One Leader	Control	**LIKE TO LIFE**	Turning Stones to Bread	Matthew 4:1-4
Surrender	Our Effort / not Faith	**DO TO DIE**	Throw yourself down	Matthew 4:5-7
Following First	Pride	**ACHIEVE TO RECEIVE**	Give you the Kingdoms	Matthew 4:8-10
Serving as Second	Self	**LEAD TO SERVE**	Serving self or others	Mark 10:45
Influencing	Secret	**FOR TO FROM**	Busy branches trying to bear fruit	John 15:5
Teamwork	Presumption	**KING TO TEAM**	Kings lord it over	Luke 22:24-30
Kingdom	Idolatry	**TEMPORAL TO ETERNAL**	Laying up Treasures	Matt 6:19-21

One Leader

This principle takes us out of the role of leader and acknowledges that Christ works through us as the true Leader in our role as steward of the process. We so often hear that we should become "like" Christ in our character and activity; instead, we should allow Christ to be our very life. This was the issue in the very first temptation of Christ when Satan tempted Him to turn stones into bread. Satan was tempting Christ to meet His own need of food after 40 days, and if He could turn stones into bread, He could meet the needs of the world and the world would follow. It was an issue of trying to be in control of circumstances and meeting needs. Jesus cut to the heart: "Man shall not live on bread alone but on every word that proceeds from the mouth of God." We need to trust God with His control, His supply, and the knowledge that He is our life. Being "like" Christ is a by-product to advertise Him to the world, not a prescription for performance or a to-do list for being a more effective leader.

Surrender

The surrender principle asserts that the Christian life is not about our doing but more about our dying. We need to get out of the way for God to work. We don't make the Christian life or maturity happen in our strength; the Lord works in our weakness. In fact, Paul indicated that it was only in His weakness that the power of Christ was made manifest. Satan was tempting Jesus to do something spectacular, to put on a big show so the world would be entertained and come to Him. Jesus simply said: "You shall not test God." It takes real faith to believe God when we can "do" something or when we are at our last thread.

Follow

The follow principle highlights that leadership is derived from a love relationship with the Lord and that we have a new identity in Him. The leader's identity is not from the things we take "pride" in: our character, influence, charisma, talents, or results. We are simply new creations in Christ, who loves us unconditionally, and we need to receive this by faith—it is not earned. Satan attempted to lure Christ by offering Him the kingdoms of the world (great influence). He flatly rejected this and said: "You shall worship the Lord your God only." So often as leaders we fall into the trap of believing that our worth and significance come from our work or outcomes rather than an intimate relationship that He gives and we need to receive. This *agape* love relationship can never be earned.

Serve

Often we have heard that "Leaders Lead." It sounds good, yet on five occasions when confronted with the disciples' question of who was the greatest, Jesus instructed them: It is the one who serves. At the heart of Jesus' teaching was the truth that the Christian life and leadership is not about "self" but all about others. Self, self-effort, and self-absorption are truly pictures of sin. Jesus modeled servant leadership, and He was the greatest leader of all time—should we do or want more? We need to put others ahead of ourselves as Paul notes in **Philippians 2:3-4**: *"Do nothing from selfishness or empty conceit but with humility of mind regard others as more important than yourself."* It will take true humility to serve others ahead of ourselves.

Influence

This temptation is probably the most subtle and difficult. We are so naturally inclined to do something *for* Christ because it is a good work, the mission helps others, we pay the Lord back, and the list goes on. It feels good and produces good results. What is hard to recognize is that central to the effort is our strength, our capacity, our getting others to do something good. God does not need us, He simply wants to work through us. We can only be in a position to be used if we are branches that are clean, available, and abiding in the vine. Jesus clearly states that apart *from* Him we can do nothing. The world glorifies leadership as influence, Christ says *He* will influence through us if we are rightly connected to the vine.

Teamwork

This principle focuses on the fact that more can be done and the work is leveraged with teams of people rather than having one person barking orders, delegating, and telling people what to do. The problem is that people prefer to hold on to power rather than empower others. This is true for many leaders—the power and significance goes to their heads, and they do most anything to hold on to it. We must realize that leaders accomplish more through people than they can in their own capacity and strengths.

Kingdom

This principle says that the goal of our life and leadership is all about God's glory and Kingdom, not about building some big organization or achieving big results in this world. If what we do does not glorify God, it is wood, hay, and stubble that will burn up (see 1 Corinthians 3:12-15). This world is not our home, and the outward products of our hands and work are temporal. The Lord is establishing His Kingdom through us in the lives of people and in heaven as we have the right motives and allow God to work through us.

SUMMARY: The One Leader principles will require you to "shift" your leadership style, motives, and way you lead. It will be challenging, yet it will be the most rewarding.

My friend Tom writes about how he moved from "achieving" in his Christian life and leadership to "receiving." It is powerful to see Christ working through a person to change his life.

> *The Lord brought me into relationship with Him later in life. I have been a believer for over 25 years now, trying to be faithful to the call, but not until a few years ago did I more fully comprehend and experience "the gospel of the grace of God" (Acts 20:24). Apparently, a driven type A personality such as myself has a fair amount of renewal to go through in order to experience true freedom in Christ.*

> *You see, I had been taught my whole life to gain approval, acceptance, significance, and love through performance. I brought that habit or "flesh pattern" right into my walk with God. ... It looks good on the surface but in the end, as I have experienced, it leads to burnout, broken marriages, and a growing lack of true intimacy with the Lord.*

A few years ago I began to see that I was living in the wilderness of self-effort, attempting to make up in speed (effort) for what I lacked in direction (grace). Actually, I began to learn that I already had all the grace I needed; as the Word says, "God's divine power has given us everything we need for life and godliness" (2 Peter 1:3). I had that verse and several others memorized and had read books that proclaimed the gospel of God's grace ... but not until I experienced divine revelation through the working of the Holy Spirit did I truly embrace the power and knowledge of God on a deep, life-changing level. I can tell you it was a real struggle because it seemed everything around me kept trying to pull me back into the hole from which God was trying to rescue me.

God was trying to show me how to work from a position of resting in Christ's sufficiency, His "easy yoke." The transformation occurred when I finally yielded my life to His life within me. A great exchange took place! I already had His power, His mind, and His person dwelling in me and me in Him. However, I was blocking His life from completely flowing through me by a futile attempt to maintain control in a willful effort to get some of my needs met apart from Him.

Christ's life living in and flowing through me by my willful submission to Him has brought forth the fruit of the Spirit, satisfaction of my soul, a healed marriage, fruitful ministry, and a more profound intimate knowledge of Him and a confidence of His great love for me. I now see this as "walking in the Spirit." As a little child of God, I needed to learn to walk all over again.

One caution. Those dark forces still desire to put me under the yoke of self-effort. ... Yet, His love has given me a free will to choose something I can do. I must continually, day by day, moment by moment, choose life...choose Christ's life, to seek His face and yield to His presence. Unspeakable joy is His offer and to God be the glory!

ONE LEADER PRINCIPLE: Leadership is a role that the Lord gives to us and we receive from Him; it begins with Christ. It is not simply a position to fill or a place where power is exercised, it is begins with the Life of Christ in us.

ONE LEADER PRAYER: (personalize this passage as a prayer to God)

"...Pray that the eyes of your heart may be enlightened, so that you will know what is the hope of His calling, what are the riches of the glory of His inheritance in the saints, 19 and what is the surpassing greatness of His power toward us who believe. These are in accordance with the working of the strength of His might 20 which He brought about in Christ..." **(Ephesians 1:8).**

ENDNOTES

1   *Spiritual Leadership* by Henry Blackaby
2   Howard G. Hendricks, noted Christian teacher and author
3   "The Cost of Discipleship" by Dietrich Bonhoffer
4   Ibid.

Section Two

APPLYING THE ONE LEADER PRINCIPLES

Chapter Five

THERE IS ONE LEADER AND YOU ARE ... NOT IT!

". . . For One is your Leader, that is, Christ" (Matthew 23:10).

WHAT GOD WANTS

If I had only one message to give to the world of leaders, it would be this—Christ lives today in the spirit of every Christian, and He wants to lead through every one of us. He does not need our grand plans or our sweat-driven performance to do big things *for* Him. God wants us to be clean, unpretentious vessels that He flows through in order to accomplish His work. Christ is the One Leader in us, and we receive from Him what we need to fulfill our roles.

This truth maybe difficult to receive because the fundamental requirements a leader needs to bring to the table are total surrender and an empty, clean vessel for His use. In other words, God does not need you or any of your efforts that come from your flesh. We all may give mental assent to this, but it takes a revelation from His Spirit for us to embrace this in our hearts.

A NEW AND DIFFERENT WAY

Let's begin by taking a look at Matthew 23. Jesus was teaching the disciples about true, biblical leadership in the last days before His death on the cross. He contrasts the leadership of the Pharisees and Scribes with a new and different way! His message addressed the need of that hour, and we have that same need today. Consider what He told His own disciples in **Matthew 23:1-12.**

"Then Jesus spoke to the crowds and to His disciples, saying: 'The scribes and the Pharisees have seated themselves in the chair of Moses; therefore all that they tell you, do and observe, but do not do according to their deeds; for they say things and do not do them. They tie up heavy burdens and lay them on men's shoulders, but they themselves are unwilling to move them with so much as a finger.

"'But they do all their deeds to be noticed by men for they broaden their phylacteries and lengthen the tassels of their garments. They love the place of honor at banquets and the chief seats in the synagogues, and respectful greetings in the market places, and being called Rabbi by men.

"'But do not be called Rabbi; for One is your Teacher, and you are all brothers. Do not call anyone on earth your father; for One is your Father, He who is in heaven. **Do not be called leaders; for One is your Leader, that is, Christ.** *But the greatest among you shall be your servant. Whoever exalts himself shall be humbled; and whoever humbles himself shall be exalted'"* (emphasis added).

Jesus' message to His disciples was that the leaders of that day held positions of influence, yet were not worthy to be followed. These men had no care or respect for people and, in fact, used them for personal gain. They loved the accolades, the places of honor, and would do anything to remain in power—power that was derived from their positions and their offices rather than in their followers' willing allegiance and appreciation.

All too often we can find ourselves acting like a Pharisee when we get caught up in our causes, trying hard to do big things for God. Many seek out positions of leadership and enjoy being in the place of power to make things happen. It can take years to peel off the layers of the world's way of leadership and transform our heart in order to lead (serve) others *for their good* rather than for our own. This transformation happens when we take hold of the life of Christ within us.

Furthermore, Jesus told His disciples that leadership was not something to be sought, to be grasped, or to be used for personal gain. He makes the bold statement that there is **only One Leader: Jesus Christ**. That means leadership *comes from Jesus Christ*. Just as all spiritual life flows from God, so all leadership flows from Jesus Christ, who is the Leader in us. True life-changing leadership does not come from our own resources but from Him and His supernatural resources. This is a radical perspective!

Here's a revolutionary thought—**we don't need more leaders!** We have the one and only Leader, Jesus Christ! **We need people who are available to let Christ live and lead in and through them as they function in their daily roles.**

The work that interests God is His work that is accomplished as He flows through us. All of our life and leadership will be tested by fire, and depending on the source of the work, it will be revealed as gold, silver, and precious stones or wood, hay, and stubble (see 1 Corinthians 3:11-15).

> *"Too often, people assume that along with the role of leader comes the responsibility of determining what should be done. They develop aggressive goals. They dream grandiose dreams. They cast grand visions. Then they pray and ask God to join them in their agenda and to bless their efforts. That is not what spiritual leaders do. Spiritual leaders seek God's will."*

> *"Jesus was never required to develop ministry goals or action plans. He was sent to follow the Father's plan to the letter. . . . The Father had already developed the plan and Jesus' responsibility was to carefully obey the Father's will."*
> Henry Blackaby[1]

We are not leaders because of our position, strength, or resources. When Christ is our life, He is the One Leader in us and we fulfill the role of leadership as Christ works through us wherever He places us. From this indwelling Spirit of Christ, our leadership focuses on fulfilling the will of God.

JESUS CHRIST AS LEADER

Jesus Christ was and still is the only true Leader! Why? In the following verses Jesus describes how He has been given **all authority** (emphasis added). Authority is the basis of leadership and it resides only in Christ and not in man. This authority was given to Him from God the Father. This authority is lived out through us as we live in an intimate relationship with Him.

*"When Jesus had finished these words, the crowds were amazed at His teaching; for He was **teaching them as one having authority**, and not as their scribes* (**Matthew 7:28-29**).

*"'But so that you may know that the **Son of Man has authority on earth to forgive sins'**—then He said to the paralytic, 'Get up, pick up your bed and go home.' And he got up and went home. But when the crowds saw this, they were awestruck, and glorified God, who had given such authority to men"* (**Matthew 9:6-8**).

*"And Jesus came up and spoke to them, saying, '**All authority has been given to Me** in heaven and on earth. Go therefore and make disciples of all the nations, baptizing them in the name of the Father and the Son and the Holy Spirit, teaching them to observe all that I commanded you; and lo, I am with you always, even to the end of the age'"* (**Matthew 28:18-20**).

We conclude that God the Father conferred upon Jesus Christ all authority. Another way of saying that Jesus Christ has all authority is that He has all leadership. God the Father and Jesus Christ are the source of all leadership!

JESUS CHRIST'S PARADIGM AND MODEL OF LEADERSHIP

When the world describes leadership, the words *strong, decisive, charismatic, skillful, bold,* and *courageous* are typically used. Leaders are self-contained and self-motivated. Some people have it and some do not. Often, we project this thinking into our arenas of influence, whether in the home or at work.

We need to set aside our view of leadership and focus on how Jesus leads. Jesus Christ was very unique in His leadership and was totally unlike the world's leaders. Reflect on what was so unusual about Jesus Christ (emphasis added).

*"Jesus gave them this answer: 'I tell you the truth, **the Son can do nothing by Himself**; He can do only what He sees his Father doing, because whatever the Father does the Son also does'"* **(John 5:19)**.

*"**I can do nothing on My own initiative**. As I hear, I judge; and My judgment is just, because I do not seek My own will, but the will of Him who sent Me"* **(John 5:30)**.

*"For I have come down from heaven, **not to do My own will**, but the will of Him who sent Me"* **(John 6:38)**.

*"So Jesus said, 'When you lift up the Son of Man, then you will know that I am He, and **I do nothing on My own initiative**, but I speak these things as the Father taught Me. And He who sent Me is with Me; He has not left Me alone, for I always do the things that are pleasing to Him'"* **(John 8:28-29)**.

*"Jesus said to them, 'If God were your Father, you would love Me, for I proceeded forth and have come from God, for **I have not even come on My own initiative**, but He sent Me"* **(John 8:42)**.

*"For **I did not speak on My own initiative**, but the Father Himself who sent Me has given Me a commandment as to what to say and what to speak"* **(John 12:49)**.

*"Do you not believe that I am in the Father, and the Father is in Me? The words that I say to you **I do not speak on My own initiative**, but the Father abiding in Me does His works"* **(John 14:10)**.

Amazingly, Christ described Himself as a "do nothing on my own" leader; it was the Father who initiated the work. **God the Father was the source of Christ's leadership, and it was transferred through an intimate relationship.** The fact that Jesus says seven times that He did not work or minister on His own direction and power is startling. Initiative is the *very* thing that leaders are supposed to show! What does this mean? How should it change our paradigm of leadership?

Jesus Christ's leadership did not depend on His own resources except that He was *totally dependent and restfully available* for the Father to use Him. This gives insight into what God desires us to be as leaders: surrendered, dependent, listening, and willing to obey.

Henry Blackaby describes this relationship:

> *"If Jesus provides the model for spiritual leadership, then the key is not for leaders to develop visions and to set direction for their organizations. The Key is to obey and to preserve everything the Father reveals to them of His will. Ultimately, the Father is the leader.*

> *"God has visions of what He wants to do. God does not ask leaders to dream big dreams for Him or to solve the problems that confront them. He asks leaders to walk with Him so intimately that, when He reveals what is on His agenda, they will immediately adjust their lives to His will and the results bring Glory to God."*[2]

LEADERSHIP WITH SEVEN RELATIONAL FACETS

Jesus Christ's leadership came out of an intimate relationship with the Father. So, too, our leadership should flow out of a dynamic, multifaceted relationship with Christ.

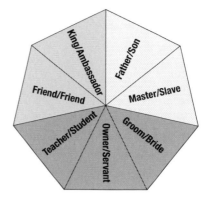

Let's look at the seven principles of the One Leader model in the context of our relationship God the Father and our Lord Jesus Christ. Observe the connection of principles, relationship, and insight.

One Leader Principles	One Leader Relational Facets	Insight
Leaders know the One Leader, Jesus Christ, and His work through them.	**Facet 1:** **Father/Son** Gal 4:1-5,7; Eph 1:5	Our leadership comes from and is defined by an intimate relationship with our Father.
Leaders release His power by brokenness and surrender.	**Facet 2:** **Master/Slave** Matt 25:14-30; Luke 19:12-27	Like the slave, we have been bought with a price, and our life is not our own. We work to please our master. It is not about us and what we are doing for God.
Leaders follow first.	**Facet 3** **Groom/Bride** Matt 25:1-13; Rev 21:2,9	Our intimate relationship with Christ should be based on our union with Him. From this place the Lord speaks to us and guides us.
Leaders serve as second.	**Facet 4:** **Owner/Servant** Phil 1:1; Romans 1:1 Matt 20:1-16	We serve the Lord with all our heart and being. We are called to do this well and faithfully.
Leaders influence to the third and fourth generations.	**Facet 5:** **Teacher/Student (Disciple)** Matt 10:24-25; John 13:5	Leadership skills can be learned, and we can grow in our effectiveness if we are disciplined. This allows us to help and serve others.
Leaders leverage best through teamwork.	**Facet 6** **Friend/Friend** John 15:13-15	The connection of a leader and his team is one of mutual trust and caring for one another. We watch the backs of our teammates.
Leaders are Kingdom-focused and leave a lasting legacy.	**Facet 7:** **King/Ambassador** 2 Cor 5:29	Leadership has a goal, focus, and impact well beyond our ability, strength, and smarts. It is all about God's Kingdom.

These relational facets will help define and direct our true leadership. We tend to focus most on perhaps one or two of these facets; yet, when the depth and breadth of these seven facets are fully realized, our leadership effectiveness will be transformed.

GOD'S LEADERSHIP

Paul gives us a very unique picture of God's leadership: *"But thanks be to God, who always leads us in triumph in Christ, and manifests through us the sweet aroma of the knowledge of Him in every place. For we are a fragrance of Christ to God among those who are being saved and among those who are perishing..."* (**2 Corinthians 2:14-16**).

A number of key insights are found in these verses.
- We are to be ***thankful*** for God's leadership; this is a starting point for leaders.
- God is ***always*** leading us, if we will humble ourselves and allow Him to work.
- We are led in ***triumph***, or victory, in Christ. This victory is available for everyone.
- God ***manifests*** Himself through us as a sweet aroma of the knowledge of Him. God shines through us as a light in the midst of darkness.
- This sweet aroma is in ***every place***. When God works through us, He also goes before us, behind us, and alongside us to influence and be an aroma.
- This fragrance is for both the believers and the seekers ***among*** us.

God's leadership in and through us changes us, promotes Himself, and furthers His Kingdom. This is infinitely greater than anything we can do for Him in our zeal and activity.

A TRUTH THAT IS REVEALED

Many in the Christian community embrace the idea that Jesus Christ, in the form of the Holy Spirit in us, should govern and guide our lives. This truth is little realized, however, because most of us receive Christ as Savior and acknowledge Him as Lord, yet we take over the control and responsibility for our daily walk.

As followers of Christ, we know we have eternal life, yet we think of it as a future state rather than a truth to be lived today. The great truth is that we have eternal life *now*. The even greater truth is that the infinite God, who created the whole universe, lives in us and desires to live through us. God is alive in us and we have all of Him. This truth is only received by revelation. Many know this principle in their minds and can quote the verse from the Bible yet never live these truths from their hearts.

Our tendency is to say: "If leadership is going to be, it must be up to me." Most people say, "Leaders take action; they don't wait, they initiate." It sounds good in the marketplace and in the boardroom, but it does not work like this in the spiritual realm. We must continually seek God's will and allow Him to work this truth out in us.

Oswald Chambers further illustrates the point:

> *"A worker without this solemn dominant note of concentration on God is apt to get his work on his neck; there is no margin of body, mind or spirit free, consequently he becomes spent out and crushed. There is no freedom, no delight in life; nerves, mind and heart are so crushingly burdened that God's blessing cannot rest. But the other side is just as true—when once the concentration is on God, all the margins of life are free and under the dominance of God alone.*

> *"There is no responsibility on you for the work; the only responsibility you have is to keep in living constant touch with God, and to see that you allow nothing to hinder your co-operation with Him."*[3]

The following reflects the power of this principle in the life and ministry of Stan, a longtime friend of mine. God used Stan to share the Gospel with me back in 1979 and helped introduce me to Jesus Christ. He shares how Christ is transforming his leadership in the marketplace ministry he oversees.

"This past January, as a part of the study, Leadership Revolution, Bruce shared with me a verse that has impacted my life and changed the local ministry. You have to know me. Simply put, I am an upfront, take-the-bull-by-the-horns type of man. I have an ego for no reason, as I am not talented, nor as smart as Bruce or as gifted as others. I only have one trait, and that is tenacity. It is not even listed as a gift or talent in Scripture, but when Bruce shares I listen.

"Matthew 23:10: 'And do not be called leader, for one is your leader, that is Jesus Christ.' Since January, I have prayed this Scripture almost every day. The results are that I must decrease and Christ must increase in the men around me. These men must take the responsibility of 'His' ministry and not just follow me, but lead with their gifts and talents.

"First and foremost in becoming a leader, I must follow Him. The entire management of the ministry is changed and changing as I write this. The men in our leadership now are empowered by the Holy Spirit. They do not have to check with the organization or me to do what God has called them to do. Having implemented this, we are becoming a movement constrained by the Holy Spirit and directed by Him alone.

"I feel out of sequence and out of control, as if I am not in charge. The reality is I have never been, but I have acted or behaved in that capacity. Those days, 14 years, are now dead…

today there is but one Leader and His name is Jesus. The result is that we are free in Christ, not constrained."

Stan Bower

ONE LEADER PRINCIPLE: Leaders know the One Leader, Jesus Christ, and His work through them. He is the Leader in us, and He works through us as we seek to follow in an intimate relationship.

ONE LEADER PRAYER: (personalize these passages as a prayer to God)

"But thanks be to God, who always leads us in triumph in Christ, and manifests through us the sweet aroma of the knowledge of Him in every place. For we are a fragrance of Christ to God among those who are being saved and among those who are perishing; 16 to the one an aroma from death to death, to the other an aroma from life to life" (**2 Corinthians 2:14-16**).

"I am the vine, you are the branches; he who abides in Me and I in him, he bears much fruit, for apart from Me you can do nothing" (**John 15:5**).

ENDNOTES

1   *Spiritual Leadership* by Henry Blackaby, page 23 by Henry Blackaby, page 23
2   Ibid.
3   *My Utmost for His Highest* by Oswald Chambers, April 23rd "Laborers together with God," 1 Corinthians 3:9

THERE IS ONE LEADER AND YOU ARE...NOT IT!

Chapter Six

BROKENNESS AND SURRENDER RELEASE THE POWER OF CHRIST

"God's Son received the highest assignment, and it culminated in a cross. Knowing and experiencing God is a progressive endeavor that depends on obedience."

Henry Blackaby[1]

True spiritual leadership displays a supernatural power and results that are far beyond the natural skills and talents of the leader. God's work is extraordinary. Yet, how does a leader begin to see this type of power? The results are what you want, yet the process is probably not what you signed up for.

CHALLENGES ARE PART OF THE PROCESS

Life always will present challenges, difficulties, and pain. These are often magnified by the schemes of the enemy, Satan, and accelerated by the lure of the world. We all must recognize that since the fall of Adam, heartache and problems are a part of life.

The Lord uses these challenges and pain to break us of our self-reliance and selfishness. Our sin is exposed and we come to the end of our resources. Brokenness is a difficult but necessary stop on the way to becoming a servant.

Yet, brokenness is not an end in itself; surrender is required on our part. In fact, brokenness is the process God uses to bring us to the end of our personal resources; we become empty. This still isn't surrender. Surrender is when we willingly and consciously choose to give up. Every true leader must go through brokenness and surrender; in other words, we must be empty of self and willing to receive in order to be filled with His Spirit.

From this surrender of ourselves, God develops our character, including the aspects of humility and integrity. As character is lived out, we mature in our attitudes and actions. We then are no longer full of ourselves and actually seek to serve others.

> *Every true leader must go through brokenness and surrender; in other words, we must be empty of self and willing to receive in order to be filled with His Spirit.*

Jesus calls each of us to a process of brokenness and surrender: *"If any man wishes to come after me, let him deny himself and take up his cross daily and follow me"* **(Luke 9:23)**. Several thoughts emerge about surrender. Surrender is a personal choice that we all have the option to make, yet this is not a one-time event—it is ongoing. The verse above indicates it's a daily process, and as we grow and mature, we realize the process is occurring moment-by-moment.

Surrender is more than just giving up and letting go. When we surrender to someone, we actually submit to their authority. For example, during the U.S. Civil War, General Robert E. Lee of the Confederate Army did not simply give up and walk away from the battle. He surrendered to General Ulysses Grant of the Union Army, who then told him the conditions of surrender. The same principle holds true for us spiritually; we surrender to Christ and follow His will and desires.

Surrender also releases the Spirit of Christ through us to others. When we are weak, Christ is made strong in us and goes to work.

BROKENNESS

God is in the reclamation business. If we are to grow and mature as leaders, we will need to recognize that God has the best plan for molding, shaping, and transforming us into vessels He can use. We must understand that He is often doing a greater work in us as we walk through life's difficulties. He has our best interests at heart and the growth process, albeit painful and lonely, is for our good and draws us into a deeper relationship with Himself.

We have the opportunity to respond by either accepting and learning or fighting and fleeing. It is in our choice whether our faith grows or diminishes, and it is in our struggle and overcoming that our character is forged, tested, and tempered. This place of dependence and weakness changes us, because we let go and commit our life and our future into God's hands. The pattern is this: God initiates and we respond.

THE BLESSING OF BROKENNESS

- Brokenness is the first step to fruitfulness (see **John 12:24**).
- Brokenness is God's means of maturing us (see **James 1:2-4**).
- Brokenness is painful, yet it is a means of ministry as we become broken bread and poured out wine (see **2 Corinthians 1:3-4**).

How is brokenness a blessing to our lives and ministry? It brings us to the end of ourselves where we need Christ to take over. It brings us to the end of our resources. It produces character. Here is a letter written by the Catholic priest, Francois Fenelon, in the 1600's, to friends held in prison. What a great challenge to each of us.

> *I cannot express to you how deeply I sympathize with you in your time of suffering. I suffer right along with you, but still, it cheers me up to know that God loves you.*
>
> *And the very proof that God loves you is that He does not spare you, but lays upon you the cross of Jesus Christ. Whatever spir-*

itual knowledge or feelings we may have, they are all a delusion if they do not lead us to the real and constant practice of dying to self. And it is true that we do not die without suffering. Nor is it possible to be considered truly dead while there is any part of us which is yet alive.

This spiritual death (which is really a blessing in disguise) is undeniably painful. It cuts "swift and deep into our innermost thoughts and desires with all their parts, exposing us for what we really are." The great Physician, who sees in us what we cannot see, knows exactly where to place the knife. He cuts away that which we are most reluctant to give up. And how it hurts! But we must remember that pain is only felt where there is life, and where there is life is just the place where death is needed.

This breaking of the outer man is central to being a leader that God can use. This idea can be seen in **Luke 9:23** where Christ tells how following Him and dying to self are tied together: *"And He was saying to them all, 'If anyone wishes to come after Me, he must deny Himself, and take up his cross daily and follow Me.'"*

Dying to self is critical for servant leadership. God desires to develop His character in every leader, and it comes through experiences of difficulty, suffering, and trials. What is critical is not the nature or severity of the difficulty but our response to it. In the following chart we see a process whereby God uses difficulty to move us to a place of brokenness and surrender, resulting in godly character a servant's heart.

Consider our response according to **James 4:10**: *"Humble yourselves in the presence of the Lord, and He will exalt you."*

Process	Truth Principle	
Life *Rewarding & Difficult* *Pain & Joy*	Life is full of difficulties, trials, and heartaches. It also has many good things. Our circumstances are where we find ourselves—good or bad.	The challenge is to embrace our day-to-day living and not allow it to subvert God as first and foremost.
Brokenness *Becoming Empty*	Life's curveballs, others' sin or my bad choices (sin) bring me to the end of myself. The Lord allows us to be tested and tried.	Being willing to give up control and allow God to rule and reign in the results. Selfish + possessiveness leads to keeping control and must be broken.
Surrender *Die to self*	A willing submission and choice to pursue God in the middle of the pain and difficulty. I come to the place of saying I can't but He can. Embrace an attitude of "follow me." Repentance.	Crucify and putting to death the flesh. Dying to self, give up, and submit our resources to God. Taking up the cross.
Character *Obedience*	Qualities include: integrity, honesty, trustworthiness, purity of heart, faithfulness, availability, teachability	Become truly and fully other-centered. Desire to build and invest in others. Seek to serve.
Maturity *Choices*	Exercising self-control and not being filled with our own desires.	Maturity gains knowledge and applies it resulting in wisdom.
Servant *Invest in others and Kingdom*	Begins to grow in maturity and exercising wisdom. Exercise the spiritual disciplines.	Have others' best interests ahead of our own.

SURRENDER

Surrender is a voluntary giving up of control and one's own effort to produce certain outcomes. These are some of the hardest things to give up, especially for leaders. Yet these are the very things that the Lord asks us to relinquish because they are not in our job description—they are God's responsibilities.

When we have surrendered to God's control and authority, we are now in a position to receive many promises from the Lord.

- There is victory in surrender – **2 Corinthians 2:14**
- Becomes a conduit of grace and love – **John 15:5**
- Brings us into community – **2 Corinthians 8:13**
- Lose your life and you will gain it – **Luke 9:23-25**
- Waiting on God (timing, guidance, and direction) – **Isaiah 40:39**
- When I am weak, He is strong – **2 Corinthians 12:9**
- Challenges become strengths as faith is tested – **James 1:2-4**

As leaders, too often we think that surrender is being weak and that others will take advantage of us. Nothing could further from the truth in the spiritual realm, because only in our surrender is the power of Christ released through us. Thus, in our humility people are inspired, they see God at work, and more can be accomplished.

People will trust you in a greater way because you are yielded to Christ; they in essence are trusting the Christ in you.

RECOGNIZE THE FLESH AND PUT IT TO DEATH

In the chart below, Nancy Leigh DeMoss[2] contrasts the difference between being a proud person and a broken person. Take time to reflect on what is in your heart and what God is saying to you. Make a check by any comment that is true for you.

Proud People	Broken People
Focus on the failure of others	Overwhelmed with a sense of their own spiritual need
A critical, fault-finding spirit; looking at everyone else's faults with a microscope, but their own with a telescope	Compassionate; can forgive much because they know how much they have been forgiven
Self-righteous; look down on others	Esteem all others better than themselves
Independent, self-sufficient spirit	Have a dependent spirit; recognize a need for others
Have to prove they are right; Claim rights; have a demanding spirit	Willing to yield the right to be right
Self-protective of their time, their rights, and their reputation	Self-denying
Desire to be served	Motivated to serve others
Desire to be a success	Motivated to make others a success
Have a drive to be recognized and appreciated	Have a sense of their own unworthiness; thrilled that God would use them at all
Wounded when others are promoted and they are overlooked	Eager for others to get the credit, rejoice when others are lifted up
Have a subconscious feeling that this ministry is privileged to have me and my gifts	Heart attitude is, "I don't deserve to have a part of this ministry"
Think of what they can do for God	Know they have nothing to offer God except Jesus flowing through their broken lives

What is the "self" that needs to die? It is not our "old nature of sin" because this died on the cross with Christ (**Romans 6:1-6**). Rather, it is our "fleshly" way of living and leading. The "flesh" could be defined as patterns of living we exercise to meet personal needs on our own terms. Two words that describe most fleshly behavior are control and doing. This realization is particularly hard for many leaders, because these behaviors are what drive them and define them. The "flesh" looks like many things: anger, selfishness, self-reliance, manipulation, or a critical spirit. By dying to self, leaders decrease and Christ increases (John 3:30).

In the chart below make a check by any fleshly traits you struggle with. The Lord wants you to recognize these issues and come to Him in confession and forgiveness, allowing Him to give you victory in the struggle.

○ ANGER	○ INADEQUATE	○ PASSIVE AGGRESSIVE
○ ANXIETY	○ FEEL REJECTED	○ PERFECTIONIST
○ ARGUMENTATIVE	○ FEEL UNWORTHY	○ PERFORMANCE-BASED
○ BOASTFUL	○ GREED	ACCEPTANCE
○ BOSSY	○ HATRED	○ PRIDE
○ COMPULSIVE	○ IDOLATRY	○ PROCRASTINATION
○ CONTROL	○ IMPATIENT	○ SELF-RELIANT
○ DECEITFUL	○ IMPULSIVE	○ SEXUAL LUST
○ DEFENSIVE	○ LAZY	○ STUBBORNNESS
○ DEMAND RIGHTS	○ MANIPULATIVE	○ SUSPICIOUS
○ DENIAL	○ MATERIALISTIC	○ TEMPER
○ ENVY	○ NERVOUSNESS	○ WORKAHOLIC
○ FEAR		○ WORRIER

A broken leader displays an inspiring humility that demonstrates a compelling modesty and is never boastful. Broken leaders do not talk about "I," "me," and "my"; rather, they focus on "we" and "us."

Broken leaders act with quiet, calm determination and rely principally on the inspiration of Christ, not charisma, to motivate. Humility creates integrity. If we are honest with ourselves we can identify many attitudes from the preceding list that we may need to address.

PRINCIPLE: *Dying to self (the putting to death the desire for power, position, possession, and pleasure) is an outward spiritual battle with the enemy, an inward tug of war with the flesh, and an ongoing push against the flow of the world.*

Brokenness involves asking ourselves the right question in our difficulties: "What can I learn?" rather than "Why is this happening?" Surrender is the choice we make to let God be God in our life.

SUMMARY: SPIRITUAL LEADERSHIP

In these two chapters we have reviewed the spiritual foundation for all leadership. This foundation consists of Christ as the One Leader, the source of life and power in our leadership. Having already received this power, it is released to work through us as we come to the end of our resources and surrender to Him.

These principles are rarely discussed and even less applied. So, let's review several ways in which we can incorporate them into our daily leadership.

1. **Begin to study, reflect and memorize verses that reveal Christ as our Life and Christ as the One Leader, which are found in Chapter Five.**
2. **Look for the work of God around you; take note of what He is doing.**
3. **Join God at work rather than trying to live and lead in your own strength.**
4. **Seek to identify fleshly patterns, confess them to the Lord, and give them over to His control.**
5. **Recognize that the challenges you currently are facing are being used by the Lord to grow your faith and teach you dependence.**
6. **Thank Him for walking with you in the trials.**

ONE LEADER PRINCIPLE: Leaders release His power by brokenness and surrender. Through this breaking process, the leadership power of Christ flows through us. Ultimately, we're called to be clean and humble.

ONE LEADER PRAYER: (personalize this passage as a prayer to God)

"And He has said to me, "My grace is sufficient for you, for power is perfected in weakness." Most gladly, therefore, I will rather boast about my weaknesses, so that the power of Christ may dwell in me. 10 Therefore I am well content with weaknesses, with insults, with distresses, with persecutions, with difficulties, for Christ's sake; for when I am weak, then I am strong" **(2 Corinthians 12:9-10).**

ENDNOTES

1 *Spiritual Leadership* by Henry Blackaby
2 *Brokenness: The Heart God Revives* by Nancy Leigh DeMoss

Chapter Seven

FOLLOWING FIRST

". . . I count all things to be loss in view of the surpassing value of knowing Christ Jesus my Lord . . ." (Philippians 3:8).

RELATIONAL LEADERSHIP

Building on the principles of Spiritual Leadership, we will next examine three principles that comprise the basis of Relational Leadership.

1. Leadership is formed by **Following First.**
2. Leadership is modeled by **Serving as Second.**
3. Leadership is expanded by **Influencing to the Third and Fourth Generations.**

"Following" focuses on our vertical or spiritual relationship with the Lord. "Serving" looks at our human relationships, including ourselves. "Influencing" relates to how we approach and accomplish tasks.

FOLLOWING – DEVELOPING THE INNER LIFE OF A LEADER

Following Christ should be every leader's absolute top priority. Following Christ is a spiritual relationship that is fostered by our growing *intimacy* with God the Father, our realizing who we are in Christ—our new *identity*, and our appropriating the life of Christ *indwelling* us through the Holy Spirit. We will look at each of these components in-depth, but let's first look at the following framework that defines each truth and lists the treasures we will discover as we grow in our relationship with Him.

91

- **Intimacy – God's love for us produces wholeness in our life and a love for others.**
  1. God's unconditional love is not earned.
  2. We are never alone.
  3. God's love for others through us is unlimited.
  4. His love meets our deepest needs.
  5. This abiding relationship produces fruit and maturity.

- **Identity – Spiritually loving ourselves gives us security, satisfaction, and significance.**
  1. We are new creations with a new heritage, family, beginning, and destination.
  2. We are free in Christ and no longer in bondage to legalism.
  3. Our needs for acceptance, security, and significance are met in Him directly or indirectly through people.
  4. It is an eternal treasure received now.

- **Indwelling – Christ's Spirit in us gives us confidence, hope, and joy.**
  1. Christ in us is our source of life, hope, wisdom, and power.
  2. Christ produces a hope in us that becomes a ministry to others.
  3. We move from trying to be "like" Christ to receiving the "life" of Christ.

FOLLOWING CHRIST RESULTS IN SPIRITUAL TRANSFORMATION AND LEADS TO MATURITY

Spiritual growth is an inside-out process of transformation. C. S. Lewis speaks of living this out:

> *"Authority exercised with humility and obedience accepted with delight are the very lines along which our spirits live. Obedience is the road to freedom, humility the road to pleasure, unity the road to personality."*

To follow is the first step to maturity. A leader should be forever growing, transforming, and maturing. Without maturity in the Lord, a spiritual leader is no better or different than a selfish, self-centered leader in the world. The Word has much to say about maturity.

"When I was a child, I talked like a child, I thought like a child, I reasoned like a child. When I became a man, I put childish ways behind me. Now we see but a poor reflection as in a mirror; then we shall see face to face. Now I know in part; then I shall know fully, even as I am fully known" **(1 Corinthians 13:11-12).**

"To prepare God's people for works of service, so that the body of Christ may be built up until we all reach unity in the faith and in the knowledge of the Son of God and become mature, attaining to the whole measure of the fullness of Christ. Then we will no longer be infants, tossed back and forth by the waves, and blown here and there by every wind of teaching and by the cunning and craftiness of men in their deceitful scheming" **(Ephesians 4:12-14).**

"I press on toward the goal to win the prize for which God has called me heavenward in Christ Jesus. All of us who are mature should take such a view of things. And if on some point you think differently, that too God will make clear to you. Only let us live up to what we have already attained" **(Philippians 3:14).**

INTIMACY BEGINS BY RECEIVING THE LOVE OF GOD

We must receive God's love before we can give it! We must receive God's love in order to be able to love Him in return. Why? God wants us more than we want Him. He paid an infinite price for us. His love fills us up and sustains us, yet we must proactively receive and pursue this relationship with the Father. This receiving and then giving process is ongoing, constantly replenishing the well from which a leader draws in order to be able to give to others.

How much does God love us? What is the nature of the love? Simply put, God loves us with an infinite love—He paid the price for our sin with the death of His Son, Jesus Christ. God gave all for us. This love has no conditions—no strings attached. It is a free gift. The implications of are beyond what we can understand or imagine. The following verses anchor these truths into our hearts and minds.

"For while we were still helpless, at the right time Christ died for the ungodly. For one will hardly die for a righteous man; though, perhaps for the good man someone would dare even to die. But God demonstrates His own love toward us, in that while we were yet sinners, Christ died for us" **(Romans 5:6-8)**.

"Who will separate us from the love of Christ? Will tribulation, or distress, or persecution, or famine, or nakedness, or peril, or sword? …But in all these things we overwhelmingly conquer through Him who loved us. For I am convinced that neither death, nor life, nor angels, nor principalities, nor things present, nor things to come, nor powers, nor height, nor depth, nor any other created thing, will be able to separate us from the love of God, which is in Christ Jesus our Lord" **(Romans 8:35, 37-39)**.

As we pursue and live in intimacy with Christ, we will realize that there is nothing we can do to have God love us more, and there is nothing we can do that will cause God to love us less. To the degree that we receive God's love and give it out, we will have either a positive or negative influence on those around us to do likewise.

Paul helps us to understand the magnitude of God's love in these verses:

"For this reason I bow my knees before the Father, from whom every family in heaven and on earth derives its name, that He would grant you, according to the riches of His glory, to be strengthened with power through His Spirit in the inner man, so that Christ may dwell in your hearts through faith; and that you, being rooted and grounded in love, may be able to comprehend with all the saints what is the breadth and length and height and depth, and to know the love of Christ which surpasses knowledge, that you may be filled up to all the fullness of God. Now to Him who is able to do far more abundantly beyond all that we ask or think, according to the power that works within us, to Him be the glory in the church and in Christ Jesus to all generations forever and ever. Amen" **(Ephesians 3:14-21)**.

MINISTERING TO THE LORD

Our first ministry is not outward but upward. Just as the priests of the Old Testament ministered *to* the Lord, we are to do the same.

"But the priests, the Levites, the sons of Zadok, that kept the charge of my sanctuary when the children of Israel went astray from me, they shall come near to me to minister unto me; and they shall stand before me to offer unto me the fat and the blood, saith the LORD God" **(Ezekiel 44:15).**

Much so-called service *for* Him is simply following our natural inclinations. We have such active dispositions that we cannot bear to stay at home, so we run around for our own relief. We may appear to be serving believers, but all the while we are serving our own flesh and self-interest.

Ministering to the Lord is worship, praise, and thanksgiving. This is the practical outworking of intimacy. It is giving back to the Lord all that we have received. The conditions basic to "ministry to the Lord" are drawing near to Him and standing before Him, because it is only as we draw near to Him that we can minister to Him. You who are leaders need to particularly consider this. Can you be persuaded to call a halt to endless activity and not move for a little while?

We also see in this passage from Acts that the Holy Spirit commissions men to His work as they are ministering to the Lord. *"As they ministered to the Lord and fasted, the Holy Ghost said: Separate me Barnabas and Saul for the work whereunto I have called them"* **(Acts 13:2).** The work of God is God's own work, and not work that you can take up on your own initiative.

Men cannot send men to work for God. The authority to commission men is not in the hands of men, but solely in the hands of the Spirit of God.

Serving the Lord does not mean that we do not serve people, but it does mean that all service to people has service to the Lord as its basis. It is service God-ward that urges us man-ward.

WE GROW IN OUR INTIMACY BY EXERCISING THE SPIRITUAL DISCIPLINES

The Spiritual Disciplines: The strength and health of the graft between the vine and the branch affects both the life of the branch and fruit of the vine. To exercise the spiritual disciplines is a part of God's invitation to become intimate with Him. As we look at the spiritual disciplines, it is imperative to know that the disciplines are not the end; they are a means to the end of loving God. Dallas Willard in *The Spirit of the Disciplines* says:

> *"The disciplines are activities of mind and body, purposefully undertaken, to bring our personality and total being into effective cooperation with the divine order. They enable us more and more to live in a power that is, strictly speaking, beyond us, deriving from the spiritual realm itself, as we 'yield ourselves to God, as those that are alive from the dead, and our members as instruments of righteousness unto God,' as Romans 6:13 puts it."*

The two primary means of exercising the spiritual disciplines are growing in God's Word and praying.

Taking the Word into Our Hearts

God's Word is more than a history book or textbook to be studied. It reveals Christ Himself. John 1:1 says, *"In the beginning was the Word and the Word was with God and the Word was God."* Later on it says that the Word became flesh—referring to Jesus Christ. So, when we interact with the Word (read, study, memorize) we are interacting with Christ. We are getting to know Him in our heart. If we do not take the Word into our heart, it is like living an active life while starving.

We take the Word into our heart in at least five ways:
- **HEAR** – Listen to people teach from the Bible – Revelations 1:3
- **READ** – Read consistently through the Bible – Revelations 1:3
- **STUDY** – Detailed examination of all truth – 2 Timothy 2:15, Acts 17:11

- **MEMORIZE** – Memorize verses/chapters – Proverbs 3:3, Psalm 119:11
- **MEDITATE** – Thoughtful and prayerful consideration – Psalm 1:2, Joshua 1:8

We should be clear about the PURPOSE of taking the Word into our hearts. It is *not for knowledge!* It is:

- To *know God the Father*/Son/Holy Spirit – John 14:23; 17:3
- Thus to *love Him* affectionately, intimately, and exclusively – John 14:21; 15:9-10
- To *understand His truth* – Luke 24:27, 45; Ephesians 1:17-18
- To *ascertain His will*; obedience – John 14:15.
- To *check what is heard and read* – Acts 17:11; Daniel 9:2
- All this is by *revelation* – it is not intellectual perception.

Prayer

Prayer is a phenomenal privilege, yet many people associate prayer with the word "boredom." It is a "yawn" word to them: "Well, I guess we'll have to pray." For others, their conception of prayer never gets beyond the level of "help" and "gimme." They resort to prayer when they want God to bail them out or fulfill their cravings.

Prayer is the prelude to all effective ministry. It has been said, "Satan laughs at our toiling, mocks our wisdom, but trembles when he sees the weakest saint on his knees." The real spiritual battle is won on the field of prayer; ministry simply claims the territory that has been gained. This prayer comes from a growing, intimate relationship with the Lord. We often are encouraged to pray in private rather than be seen by others.

When prayer is overlooked or appended as an afterthought to service, the power of God is often absent. It is dangerously easy to move away from dependence upon God and to slip into the trap of self-reliance.

"True godliness engages our affections and awakens within us a desire to enjoy God's presence and fellowship. It produces

a longing for God Himself. This is the heartbeat of the godly person. As he contemplates God in the awesomeness of His infinite majesty, power, and holiness, and then as he dwells upon the riches of His mercy and grace poured out at Calvary, his heart is captivated by this One who could love him so. He is satisfied with God alone, but he is never satisfied with his present experience of God. He always yearns for more."

Jerry Bridges[1]

IDENTITY – WHO AM I IN GOD'S EYES?

Knowing our identity in Christ is the second element of "following," yet in some ways it's the most profound because it's so often overlooked.

When we come into this personal relationship with God through trusting in who Christ is and what He has done for us, we move from the family of Adam to the family of God. We are adopted into this new family. What is significant about being an adopted child rather than a "natural-born" child? Adoption is a relationship of choice; it is a selection. In the Christian's case, it is God's choice. We are not an "accident" or, worse, unwanted. When God says we are adopted into His family, it means we have gained a new identity, a new heritage, and a new future.

"We are constantly in danger of letting the world define us instead of God, because it is so easy to do. It is only natural to shape our self-image by the attitudes and opinions of our parents, our peer groups, and our society. None of us are immune to the distorting effects of performance-based acceptance, and we can falsely conclude that we are worthless or that we must try to earn God's acceptance.

"It is only when we define ourselves by the truths of the Word rather than the thinking and experiences of the world that we can discover our deepest identity."

Ken Boa[2]

It is extremely important to receive the truth of what *God* says about who we are. ***Our Identity in Christ is a truth that will define us, shape us, and then compel us.*** Too often we believe the lies of the world and the enemy, all of which can have disastrous effect.

Often leaders come from difficult backgrounds and have poor relationships with their fathers, resulting in a lack of self-worth. This deficiency often becomes a driving force in their lives in order to prove to their fathers, themselves, or the world that they are somebody. Their need for approval and significance is met only through achieving some great result, whether it is in the world or even in the ministry.

When one's identity in Christ defines a person's self-worth, then the results honor God not self, the motives and values becomes other-centered, and the source of power is derived from Christ and not a desire to prove themselves.

Examine the list below. Reflect on who God says you are—your new identity.

Who I Am In Christ from God's Perspective

I am accepted...	
John 1:12	I am God's child.
John 15:15	As a disciple, I am a friend of Jesus Christ.
Romans 5:1	I have been justified.
1 Corinthians 6:19-20	I have been bought with a price, and I belong to God.
1 Corinthians 12:27	I am a member of Christ's body.
Ephesians 1:3-8	I have been chosen by God and adopted as His child.
Colossians 1:13-14	I have been redeemed and forgiven of all my sins.
Colossians 2:9-10	I am complete in Christ.
Hebrews 4:14-16	I have direct access to the throne of grace through Jesus Christ.

I am secure...	
Romans 8:1-2	I am free from condemnation.
Romans 8:28	I am assured that God works for my good in all circumstances.
Romans 8:31-39	I cannot be separated from the love of God.
2 Corinthians 1:21-22	I have been established, anointed, and sealed by God.
Colossians 3:1-4	I am hidden with Christ in God.
Philippians 1:6	I am confident that God will complete the good work He started in me.
Philippians 3:20	I am a citizen of heaven.

I am significant...	
John 15:5	I am a branch of Jesus Christ, the true vine, and a channel of His life.
John 15:16	I have been chosen and appointed to bear fruit.
1 Corinthians 3:16	I am God's temple.
2 Corinthians 5:17-21	I am a minister of reconciliation for God.
Ephesians 2:10	I am God's workmanship.
Ephesians 3:12	I may approach God with freedom and confidence.
Philippians 4:13	I can do all things through Christ, Who strengthens me.

Knowing who we are "in Christ" will dramatically change us as we accept these truths by faith. We are no longer under condemnation; rather, we are infinitely valuable because God the Father paid a price, Jesus Christ's life, for us. This is who we are from God's viewpoint. It is not a matter of trying harder or doing something for Jesus to gain acceptance. It is resting and trusting in what God has already done for us.

"Christ's limitless resources meet our deepest needs and overcome the human dilemma of loneliness, insignificance, and meaningless. When these truths begin to define our self-image,

they make us secure enough to love others without seeking our own interests first. Because of our security and significance in Christ, we do not need to be controlled by the opinions and responses of others. We have nothing to prove because we know who and whose we are. Rather than trying to impress and manipulate people, we can do our work with excellence as unto the Lord. The more we are concerned with what God thinks of us, the less we will be worried about what others think of us. And when we are no longer enslaved to people's opinion of us, we are free to love and serve them as Christ loved us—with no strings attached."

Ken Boa[3]

SUMMARY: Christ's love and acceptance gives me security, significance, and satisfaction.

- My worth and significance are found solely in Christ (which is forever and unchanging) and not in performance or in a position.
- Because of my worth in Christ, I am free from the opinions of others, though I can listen and learn from them.
- In this freedom from opinions, I can truly serve, love, value, and honor people.
- Because of my security in Christ, I can be process-focused vs. results-oriented or bottom-line driven.
- Because of this freedom I possess, I can give away power or empower others, boldly and confidently.
- "In Christ" I am free from the bondage to sin. That means I am free from one of the chief sins: pride. I need not "think more highly of myself than I ought."
- His love and acceptance gives me a security that helps me examine and purify my motives.

Without a secure identity, we will use or manipulate people for our gain. We are to live and lead from a new beginning, a new family, a new heritage, a new life, and a new inheritance. The wealth of our being in Christ will guide our walk with Him. Read the following devotional by David Wilkerson.

Christ is the treasure chest in the field. And in Him, I've found all that I'll ever need. No more trying to find purpose in ministry. No more looking for fulfillment in family or friends. No more needing to build something for God, or to be a success, or to feel useful. No more keeping up with the crowd, or trying to prove something. No more searching for ways to please people. No more trying to think or reason my way out of difficulties.
I've found what I'm looking for. My treasure, my pearl, is Christ. And all that the Owner asks of me is, "David, I love you. Let me adopt you. I've already signed the papers with my own Son's blood. You're now a joint heir with him of everything I possess."

What a bargain. I give up my filthy rags of self-reliance and good works. I lay aside my worn-out shoes of striving. I leave behind my sleepless nights on the streets of doubt and fear. And in return, I am adopted by a King. This is what happens when you seek the pearl, the treasure, till you find Him. Jesus offers you everything He is. He brings you joy, peace, purpose, and holiness. And He becomes your everything—your waking, your sleeping, your morning, afternoon, and evening.[4]

As leaders, when our identity is certain and acted upon, we exhibit a sense of being secure, significant, and satisfied. The implications of such are profound—we can walk and lead in faith without fear. We are marked by faith and not fear, which God provides for us in this new identity, and with it comes an assurance that we will never be separated from the love of God. We are always children of God, and we will never be taken away from this relationship with Christ.

Read these passages from the book of Ephesians. This is the truth of what God says about you.

- I have been blessed with every spiritual blessing in the heavenly places. **Ephesians 1:3**
- I am chosen, holy, and blameless before God. **Ephesians 1:4**
- I am redeemed and forgiven by the grace of Christ. **Ephesians 1:7**
- I have been predestined by God to obtain an inheritance. **Ephesians 1:10-11**
- I have been sealed with the Holy Spirit of promise. Ephesians 1:13
- Because of God's mercy and love, I have been made alive with Christ. **Ephesians 2:4-5**
- I am seated in the heavenly places with Christ. **Ephesians 2:6**
- I am God's workmanship created to produce good works. **Ephesians 2:10**
- I have been brought near to God by the blood of Christ. **Ephesians 2:13**
- I am a member of Christ's body and a partaker of His promise. **Ephesians 3:6; 5:30**
- I have boldness and confident access to God through faith in Christ. **Ephesians 3:12**
- My new self is righteous and holy. **Ephesians 4:24**
- I was formerly darkness, but now I am light in the Lord. **Ephesians 5:8**

THE INDWELLING LIFE OF CHRIST – CHRIST IN US IS THE "POWER FOR LIVING AND LEADING"

The third key of "following" is Christ living in us. In ourselves, we do not have the power to live the Christian life. Does that mean it's a hopeless pursuit? Absolutely not! If being "in Christ" defines who I am and gives me hope, security, and acceptance, "Christ living in me" becomes the source of life, power, and wisdom from which I can live the Christian life. The writers of the New Testament used the terms "the indwelling Holy

Spirit" and "Christ in us" interchangeably. Christ lives in us through this indwelling Spirit. Reflect on the quotes from these men of God.

> *"Good works are not produced by the Christian, but good works are borne in the life of the Christian by the Holy Spirit (Galatians 5:22-23). We are fruit-bearers not fruit-producers. Grace works out the life of Christ in us. Saving faith has intrinsic power to produce fruit."*
>
> John Piper[5]

> *"It is Christ living through us that is the secret of victorious Christian living. It is not us living for Jesus, but Jesus living through us. Failure to understand this simple truth is at the root of all legalism and the performance mentality. The law focuses on the outer man and tells it what it must do. Grace focuses on the inner man and tells it what is already done through Christ. Those who are focused on what they must do are under law. Those who are focused on what Christ has done for them are walking under grace.*

> *"Just as the life of a root is found in the soil, or a branch in the vine, or a fish in the sea, so the believer's true life is found to be in union with Christ. The Christian life is not just hard to live; it's impossible in our human strength. The only way to walk in victory is to let Christ live through us."*
>
> Dan Stone[6]

Jesus taught this message in John 14:20: *"you in Me, and I in you."* The "you in me" refers to our relationship with Christ by virtue of our life coming from Him. The "I in you" speaks of our fellowship with Christ by virtue of His life in us. The former relates to our position or standing; the latter relates to our practice or state. Our relationship with God is actual— it was determined by our spiritual *birth* in Christ. Our fellowship with God is potential—it is developed by our spiritual *growth* in Christ.

Christ Is Our Life

The Bible describes on many occasions that Christ is our life. Take note of the following verses and consider what they say about the source and substance of our life.

> *"Your real, new self (which is Christ's and also yours, and yours just because it is His) will not come as long as you are looking for it. It will come when you are looking for Him. . . . Give up yourself. And you will find your real self. Lose your life and you will save it. . . . Keep back nothing. Nothing that you have not given away will ever be really yours. Nothing in you that has not died will ever be raised from the dead. Look for yourself and you will find in the long run only hatred, loneliness, despair, rage, ruin, and decay. But look for Christ and you will find Him, and with Him everything else will be thrown in."*
>
> C. S. Lewis[7]

"For to me, to live is Christ, and to die is gain" (**Philippians 1:21**).

"The thief comes only to steal and kill and destroy; I came that they may have life, and have it abundantly" (**John 10:10**).

"For you have died and your life is hidden with Christ in God. When Christ, who is our life, is revealed, then you also will be revealed with Him in glory" (**Colossians 3:3-4**).

"Jesus said to him, "I am the way, and the truth, and the life; no one comes to the Father but through Me" (**John 14:6**).

"This is eternal life that they know me..." (**John 17:3**).

> *"If we define the concept of Christ 'living through us' as the process of receiving and displaying His indwelling life, this fits well with a number of texts, including the allegory of the vine and the branches in John 15. As we abide in Him and He abides in us, we are receiving His life rather than creating our own independent life. We draw our biological and spiritual life from*

Him, but this by no means eliminates our personalities or character development.

"The movement from position to practice is the most difficult aspect of the spiritual life. Our hearts have become Christ's dwelling place, and this truth grows more real in our awareness and experience as we lay hold of it by faith. (Ephesians 3:17)"

Ken Boa[8]

Following Bears Fruit

Fruit is the overflow of our relationship with Christ. He produces fruit in us that has both quality and quantity. We participate in the process and play a role, yet God is the source of the fruit.

As we look at John 15:1-5, we see Jesus talking about the relationship of the vine to the branch. He also connects this relationship to fruit. There is a distinct spiritual process the Lord uses to bring each of us to a greater level of fruitfulness.

We see five levels of fruit-bearing in which we can live. They comprise a spiritual process that moves us from one level to the next. Our focus should be on the process the Lord is using with us rather than quantifying or measuring the fruit. Fruit is the overflow. The key is to see the process and desire to grow in it. We realize that we do not just stay at one level. We can move up and down the levels depending on how we are living and responding to circumstances.

Let's examine John 15:1-5.

"I am the true vine, and My Father is the vinedresser. Every branch in Me that does not bear fruit, He takes away; and every branch that bears fruit, He prunes it so that it may bear more fruit. You are already clean because of the Word which I have spoken to you. Abide in Me, and I in you. As the branch cannot bear fruit of itself unless it abides in the vine, so neither can you unless you abide in Me. I am the vine, you are the branches; he who abides in Me and I in him, he bears much fruit, for apart from Me you can do nothing."

Level	Amount of Fruit	Process it takes to move to the next level
Level 1	No Fruit – John 15:2	Chastisement/correcting sin – John 15:2
Level 2	Fruit – John 15:2	Pruning – John 5:2
Level 3	More Fruit – John 15:2	Abiding in Christ – John 15:4-5
Level 4	Much Fruit – John 15:5	Invest in Others – John 15:8, 12-13
Level 5	Lasting Fruit – John 15:16	Fruit that multiplies and sustains itself – John 15:6

Bear in mind that "fruit" can have various meanings in Scripture:

- Fruit of new life – **John 15:8**
- Fruit of the Spirit – **Galatians 5:22-23**
- Fruit of righteousness – **Philippians 1:11**

Being fruitful is important in being a leader because it glorifies God, it helps others, and it expands the Kingdom. It is not for glorifying you as the leader of an organization or family.

Quit trying to be LIKE Jesus, He already is your LIFE.

What do I mean by that statement above? Are we not called to be conformed to the image of God?

We have the fullness of Christ in the form of the Holy Spirit in us from the moment of salvation. We have all of Him in us. The Christian life is not trying harder or doing something in order to look like Christ. He is to be released through my

> *"Spiritual leaders work within a paradox, for God calls them to do something that, in fact, only God can do. Ultimately spiritual leaders cannot produce spiritual change in people; only the Holy Spirit can accomplish this. Yet the Spirit often uses people to bring spiritual growth in others."*
> **Henry Blackaby**[9]

life, my actions, and my thoughts. My life will look more like Christ to the outside world as I yield to Him and walk in dependence. My focus is in *not* imitating Christ—it is releasing Him and His work through me.

In *Spiritual Leadership* Henry Blackaby challenges us to shift our paradigm: *"Our 'best thinking' will not build the Kingdom of God. Spiritual leaders must reject human reasoning in favor of God's infinite wisdom and allow Him to reveal His plans."*

We do not need more of our effort as a leader; rather, we need less of ourselves for Christ to be the One Leader in us. We must move from our focus on "CHRISTLIKE" leadership to "CHRIST LIFE" leadership. Being Christlike implies that it is up to me to be like Jesus—think like Him, act like Him, etc.

The nature of true leadership is not derived from our efforts, our motivation, and our wisdom. It flows from the resources of Christ's Life in us. This leadership functions from Him being the source, the power, and the essence.

> *"Wherever you go, God is sending you. Wherever you are, God has put you there; He has a purpose in your being there. Christ, who indwells you, has something He wants to do through you right where you are. Believe this and go in His grace, love, and power. Amen."*
>
> **Dick Halverson**[10]

We have the same power as Christ because He lives in us! This power is infinitely greater than any power we possess in ourselves or through our positions or organizations. The challenge for leaders is not to confuse the two and rely solely on their own resources.

My life and walk with the Lord were profoundly impacted by Major Ian Thomas. I remember him speaking to a conference of leaders in Colorado Springs when he used the following illustration.

> *"How much can you do without Him? Nothing! It is amazing how busy you can be doing nothing! Did you ever find that out? 'The flesh'—everything that you do apart from Him—'profiteth*

nothing' (John 6:63), and there is always the awful possibility, if you do not discover this principle, that you may spend a lifetime in the service of Jesus Christ doing nothing! You would not be the first, and you would not be the last—but that, above everything else, we must seek to avoid!

"So you discover that the life which you possess as a born-again Christian is of Him, and it is to Him, and every moment that you are here on earth it must be through Him—of Him, through Him, to Him all things! 'I beseech you therefore, brethren, by the mercies of God, that ye present your bodies a living sacrifice' (Romans 12:1).

"The Lord Jesus Christ claims the use of your body, your whole being, your complete personality so that as you give yourself to Him through the eternal Spirit, He may give Himself to you through the eternal Spirit, that all your activity as a human being on earth may be His activity in and through you; that every step you take, every word you speak, everything you do, everything you are, may be an expression of the Son of God, in you as man.

"If it is of Him and through Him and to Him, where do you come in? You do not! That is just where you go out! That is what Paul meant when he said, 'For me to live is Christ' (Philippians 1:21). The only Person whom God credits with the right to live in you is Jesus Christ; so reckon yourself to be dead to all that you are apart from what He is, and alive unto God only in all that you are because of what He is (Romans 6:11).

"It is for you to BE—it is for Him to DO! Rest fully available to the Saving Life of Christ."[11]

"It is not difficult for man to live the Christian life," somebody once said, "it is a sheer impossibility!" A sheer impossibility, that is, without *Christ*; but for all that He says, you have all that He is, and that is all that it takes!

The following is from a young man in his thirties whom I have had the privilege of mentoring over the last several years. I have known Caleb as a child and have seen him grow up. How exciting to see God work in changing a young man. Here is Caleb's leadership story in his words.

> *"As I'm sure is a common theme in many people's lives, my leadership journey began with an incredible period of broken-ness that dropped me to my knees in surrender to God's will. For years, I tried doing life my way, which led to a constant state of trouble, fear, anxiety, addiction, and unrest. It wasn't until God took most of everything I had away from me to see that my way was the wrong way, and God has had my best in-terests at heart all along. As painful as the journey was, looking back I am in awe at the work God did in my life that brought me to a place where I realized that my love, joy, and peace comes only through Christ.*

> *"However, in the beginning, trying to live this new lifestyle was very confusing. I really didn't grasp what it meant to have my identity through Christ. At this time, I started meeting with a small group of men that got together to walk through the principles of Leadership Revolution. In this group we talked through several different principles of leading through and in God's power. It turns out that one of the principles we dis-cussed is that of God's Provision. The basis of this principle is that we take hold of an identity through Christ, and in doing so we gain security, satisfaction, and significance.*

"This principle started to become real to me as I entered into the workplace. Part of my job duties in sales is to host events, meetings, and gatherings. I was very good at this and was usually the person that people turned to when they wanted to 'have a good time' and 'cut loose.' I developed the reputation of party planner within my organization and gained a tremendous amount of identity and significance through this.

"After turning from the lifestyle that went along with this reputation, I was scared that people would have no reason to come to me any more and that I would be an outcast. Honestly, part of that became a reality, but at the same time I was learning who God is and how much He loves me and it stopped mattering to me. A very close friend was casually talking to me and said, 'It shouldn't matter what people think of us—it should only matter what God thinks. When we act in a way that pleases God, what does it matter what other people think?' Exactly! I was learning to get my significance through Christ and no longer felt the need to get it from peer acceptance. What an amazing sense of freedom comes from this!

"It's been a slow process, but since then I have had a few people approach me and ask for advice on different areas of life, such as marriage. At first I was a little shocked, but realized that God was in control and doing His work through me and I didn't even realize it. Pretty amazing what can happen when we surrender our will to His and let Him work in us!"

One of the most practical applications for leaders to *follow* is to immerse themselves in the living Word, Christ, and let Him change them from the inside out!

LEADERSHIP FROM THE WORD

Watson, a dear friend and follower of Christ, has been in one of my leadership equipping teams for the last several years. He has had a true heart to know Christ and let Him be real in His life. Here is his story.

"The source of humility is knowing the source of our strength, power, and ability to forgive and impart grace. I have continued to learn, 'this source (God and His Word) is the foundation of our joy and thankfulness that sets the tone for all we do for how we lead.' In the sixth year of my job, I find myself in a much different place than what I expected.

"My expectations were: Owner with a six-figure salary; No debt; Coasting with steady book of business. Visionary and Leader for the next growth phase of the firm.

"My current reality: Employee (rank and file); Five figure salary; $100,000 in debt; Working harder than ever before; Reevaluating/Questioning what and how I am doing in a job I thought would come easy.

"I feel failure and inadequacy. I feel slighted and passed over leading to envy. So in this current state how can I lead? How can one be respected and followed if one is not successful, much less one who has a hard heart. In order to lead I need money, status, seniority, aptitude, things, etc., right? My state of mind and circumstances do not justify being a leader so how could I?

"What has been revealed to me is that my mandate for leadership was skewed. The mandate I had been given had everything to do with success defined by the world. And if that is the case I had been looking for affirmation and strength from man—not from God. But with God I already have a mandate

and justification through the redemptive blood of Christ and His call on my life.

"Here is where Leadership from the Word has had a deep impact on my life. The Word and not the world defines my success and is the source of affirmation. 'I am the vine and you are the branches...apart from me you can do nothing.' Indeed, apart from the Lord, I cannot lead.

"When Jesus sent His disciples on before Him to cross the Sea of Galilee, they were besieged by deep doubts of their direction, ability to stand in the gap with Jesus, and navigate through storms. On one occasion, they cite their inability to find bread (manna) for God's people as reason to return home. Then Jesus appears and smacks them in the jaw with this question, 'Do you still not understand?' It is not about manna nor about what you provide but about Me and my Father. It is about your trust in the Vine. From here, you can do ALL things—you can lead in humility, joy, and thankfulness by being confident in the source of your strength, power, and ability. This is all the endorsement you need to lead and lead well.

"My current circumstances are exactly where I am supposed to be. The fulfillment of my expectations would have elevated the role of the world and of me in my life. It would have separated me from the firm foundation of the Spirit/the Vine that God has given to me. I will not lead motivated by manna, but by the Spirit and the pursuit of righteousness that is by faith. Now I can lead my family, my wife, my three girls, my neighbors, and my coworkers with a humble confidence. While maybe I am not successful in the eyes of the world right now (for the record that is still very tough to speak!), I am in the eyes of God and my family and those closest to me."

Following Christ as a leader is the foundation for growth, effectiveness, and eternal fruit. Apart from this abiding love, we are only stirring up dust.

ONE LEADER PRINCIPLE: Leaders follow first. In our new identity, gift of salvation, and love for Him, our first action is to follow Jesus Christ.

ONE LEADER PRAYER: (personalize these passages as a prayer to God)

"But in all these things we overwhelmingly conquer through Him who loved us. For I am convinced that neither death, nor life, nor angels, nor principalities, nor things present, nor things to come, nor powers, nor height, nor depth, nor any other created thing, will be able to separate us from the love of God, which is in Christ Jesus our Lord" **(Romans 8:37-39)**.

"For this reason I bow my knees before the Father, from whom every family in heaven and on earth derives its name, that He would grant you, according to the riches of His glory, to be strengthened with power through His Spirit in the inner man, so that Christ may dwell in your hearts through faith; and that you, being rooted and grounded in love, may be able to comprehend with all the saints what is the breadth and length and height and depth, and to know the love of Christ which surpasses knowledge, that you may be filled up to all the fullness of God. Now to Him who is able to do far more abundantly beyond all that we ask or think, according to the power that works within us" **(Ephesians 3:14-20)**.

ENDNOTES

1   *The Practice of Godliness* by Jerry Bridges
2   *Conformed to His Image* by Ken Boa
3   Ibid.
4   "The Bride of Christ," David Wilkerson, Facebook
5   *The Pleasures of God* by John Piper
6   *The Rest of the Gospel* by Dan Stone
7   *Mere Christianity*, by C. S. Lewis
8   Op. Cit., Boa
9   *Spiritual Leadership* by Henry Blackaby, p. 21
10   former chaplain of the U.S. Senate
11   *The Saving Life of Christ* by Major Ian Thomas, Grand Rapids: Zondervan Publishing House. ©1961.

Chapter Eight

SERVING AS SECOND

". . . Give preference to one another in honor" (Romans 12:10).

When Christ discusses leadership, He puts it in the context of serving. To serve, it is necessary to put yourself in second place, placing God and others ahead of yourself. Being second is radical because we live in a culture that venerates being a winner, being first—this is not God's way.

To understand serving we will consider three primary ideas:
1. Serving begins with character
2. Serving is Valuing People
3. Serving is Being on Mission

SERVING BEGINS WITH CHARACTER.

One of the greatest challenges for us as leaders is for our "walk" to match our "talk." In other words, the character of a leader is a reflection of our following Christ. Many leaders talk a good game, yet examine their fruit and you will see what is really on the inside. This challenge is found in corporations, in the home, in the church, and in each of our individual lives.

Christ calls each us of to serve in the context of where He has placed us. Servanthood only comes from a heart of character that is filled with humility, care, and putting others first. We serve because of who God is in us not by what we are trying to do for Him. Where does character come from?

PRINCIPLE: God's process of molding us begins with a view that God always has our best interests at heart, He is never unaware and is forever in control. He is shaping us outwardly to who we are inwardly. He wants us to work out what He is working in.

> *"God will develop your character to match your assignment. God does not give big things to little character. What is God doing to develop your character? What you become, God can pass it on, you can't pass on what you don't possess."*
> **Henry Blackaby**[1]

Godly Character

It is helpful to know and understand what godly character looks like. The following are specific and concrete ways to express it.

- **Trustworthiness** – Be honest • Don't deceive, cheat or steal • Be reliable—do what you say you'll do • Have the courage to do the right thing • Build a good reputation • Be loyal—stand by your family, friends, and country.
- **Respect** – Treat others with respect; follow the Golden Rule • Be tolerant of differences • Use good manners and edifying language • Be considerate of the feelings of others • Don't threaten, hit, or hurt anyone • Deal peacefully with anger, insults, and disagreements.
- **Responsibility** – Faithful, available, and teachable • Do what you are supposed to do • Persevere: never give up! • Always do your best • Use self-control • Be self-disciplined • Think before you act—consider the consequences • Be accountable for your choices.
- **Caring** – Be kind • Be compassionate and show you care • Express gratitude • Forgive others • Help people in need.

The nature of character in our lives is an obedient heart. It is a desire to BE pleasing to God and to DO the will of God in all things. This obedience does not come from sheer willpower but from our love relationship with Christ. Jesus expresses this in John 14:21, *"He who has my commandments and keeps them is he who loves Me."* This is significant because it keeps us grounded to the fact that behavior and obedience come from a love relationship. It is not the other way around. The Christian life is not one of duty and performance that produces love. A love relationship results in goodness and fruit.

> *"True obedience is not gritting your teeth and 'doing the right thing.' It is cooperating with the breaking forth of Christ's life within....Within every believer, the desire to do the will of God is the gift of God. This desire is there because the Holy Spirit now dwells in every believer."*[2]

Character That Turns into Thankfulness

As leaders encounter difficulties in life, they move to a place of brokenness and then exercise the choice of surrender. The Lord is always working to bring us to this point so He can be the One Leader. The result of this process is an inner thankfulness and an outward serving of others.

Thankfulness is more than a positive mental attitude; it is the recognition of God's working in one's life for their good and for His glory. Thankfulness is the most practical step of faith that we as followers of Christ can take. And we are called to *"give thanks in everything"* (1 Thessalonians 5:18). In addition, this gratitude helps give each one of us perspective.

SPIRIT-LED SERVING

The source of serving begins with Christ's indwelling Spirit, who supernaturally serves and values others as God works His plan, rather than people doing something they are *supposed* to do. This Spirit-led serving transforms leaders and transcends the typical view of a servant leader. Spirit-led serving helps others for their good, values them, and accomplishes the work. This serving keeps the true end in mind: Glorifying God and being Kingdom focused.

SERVING IS MARKED BY RELATIONAL VALUES – LEADERS VALUE PEOPLE OVER TASKS

From a godly character come godly values that begin with serving and valuing others. Spiritual leaders are servant leaders who are other-centered and have healthy relationships with the people they lead. The basis for relationships is found in the Great Commandment (Matthew 22:37) and the New Commandment (John 13:34-35). Both are relational in nature—our relationship with God and with others.

Why is God so interested in healthy relationships? It is because He is relational in nature (the Trinity is the basis for all relationships), and He made us as relational beings. Having been made in His image reflects this relational capacity.

God also established the church, which is fundamentally all about relationships. The following verses underscore the meaning and value of relationships.

"Be devoted to one another in brotherly love; give preference to one another in honor; not lagging behind in diligence, fervent in spirit, serving the Lord; rejoicing in hope, persevering in tribulation, devoted to prayer, contributing to the needs of the saints, practicing hospitality" (**Romans 12:9-14**).

"Make my joy complete by being of the same mind, maintaining the same love, united in spirit, intent on one purpose. Do nothing from selfishness or empty conceit, but with humility of mind regard one another as more important than yourselves; do not merely look out for your own personal interests, but also for the interests of others. Have this attitude in yourselves which was also in Christ Jesus" (**Philippians 2:2-5**).

"Having so fond an affection for you, we were well-pleased to impart to you not only the gospel of God but also our own lives, because you had become very dear to us" (**1 Thessalonians 2:8**).

One of the most significant challenges a leader has to balance is the connection of results, process, and people. When relationships are not a priority, the tendency is to focus on results (growing bigger, better, and faster). This can lead to using people rather than valuing and serving them.

> *"The primary purpose of spiritual leaders is not to achieve their goals but to accomplish God's will. Max DuPree says, 'Reaching goals is fine for an annual plan. Only reaching one's potential is fine for a life.' Leaders can achieve goals and yet be out of God's will. Reaching goals is not necessarily a sign of God's blessing. Spiritual leaders do not use their people to accomplish their goals, the people are the goal. Spiritual leaders have a God-given responsibility to do all they can to lead their people on to God's agenda."*
>
> **Henry Blackaby**[3]

Leaders are called to a role of oversight and management of people. (This is especially true for leaders of families.) In these roles, leaders need to care for and look out for the best interests of the people they serve. In fact, their leadership should reflect loving one another unconditionally. Other biblical terms would include blessing others, being devoted to others, helping, generous giving, loving without hypocrisy, and entering into another's world. Henri Nouwen, a priest who left Harvard to shepherd a community of mentally handicapped men, gives us insight into what true caring should look like.

> *"Care is the participation in the pain, sharing the suffering and brokenness. Cure without care is as dehumanizing as a gift given with a cold heart.*
>
> *"Care means to be present to each other. They listen to you, they speak to you, they ask questions of you. Their presence is a healing presence because they accept you on your terms.*

Our tendency is to run away from the painful realities or to try to change them as soon as possible. But cure without care makes us into rulers, controllers, manipulators, and prevents a real community from taking shape. Cure without care makes us preoccupied with quick changes, impatient, and unwilling to share each other's burden."[4]

Caring at this level takes sacrifice and commitment. We need to care for people rather than try to fix their problems. When this caring is lived out, it will include rejoicing and crying for one another as Paul says in **Romans 12:15,** *"Rejoice with those who rejoice, and weep with those who weep."*

This verse speaks to the idea that we are to enter into one another's joys and sorrows, identifying with their emotions and situations. Usually the rejoicing is easy, but entering into another's pain is difficult. We are called to look beyond ourselves—not just to give logical solutions, advice, or counsel, but also to empathize and hurt with others. The key is not allowing others to go through pain *alone*—thus the need for developing community. In addition, sharing the pain carries a message for the one going through it. We, as leaders, can help others hear from the Lord.

COMMUNITY IS THE BRIDGE BETWEEN INTIMACY AND MINISTRY

"Beneath all our problems there are desperately hurting souls that must find the nourishment only community can provide or die. The greatest need in modern civilization is the development of communities—true communities where the heart of God is home, where the humble and wise learn to shepherd those on the path behind them, where trusting strugglers lock arms with others as together they journey on."

Larry Crabb[5]

In **Luke 6:12-19**, we see the flow of God's Spirit working from Intimacy to Community to Ministry. At night, Jesus is alone praying with the Father, seeking guidance in the calling of His disciples. This critical juncture in Jesus' ministry needed God's direction that only comes from intimacy. In the morning, after hearing from the Father, Jesus calls the disciples to Himself. They spend time together. This fellowship could also be described as community. Later in the day they descend from the mountain to begin to minister and to heal people. See the progression:

> **Night: alone with God, prayer, intimacy with God = INTIMACY**
> **Morning: gathered the men, a team, people focus = COMMUNITY**
> **Afternoon: went out to the world, heal disease, work = MINISTRY**

Intimacy

Intimacy is being with God and God alone. Is there any space for that in your life? How intimate are you with Christ? What about your prayer life? We need to be *deep* in our relationship with God—it's our top priority. This is the well from which we must drink in order that our life would flow to others as described in John 7:37-38. This is both our greatest joy and our greatest challenge. Intimacy found in solitude forms an initial anchor, one pillar of the bridge. It is in my aloneness with God that I know I am "beloved." If I don't understand this, I will manipulate people and situations to reach my goals or I will take credit for ministry that God has done.

Ministry

This is the other side of the bridge. The cause of the Gospel is our second anchor to keep us on track. In practical terms, ministry is evangelism and discipleship. It is helping people know Christ and grow in Him. Ministry focuses on entering into God's Kingdom purposes.

Community

Community is the bridge that connects intimacy with God together with the ministry of God. People not only deliver the Gospel, we live it out day by day. It is how we handle our difficulties and how we deal with and love people, and through which the world knows that we are His disciples (see John 13:34-35). As we experience God's acceptance, the healing of hurts, and true forgiveness, we begin to develop love that shines as light in the darkness and brings the dawning of a new day for others and ourselves. This is the bridge that takes courage to walk across; there are no short cuts. Community holds intimacy and ministry together as it loves and values people.

SERVING IS BEING PURPOSEFUL

Most people spend more time planning their next vacation than they do the purpose of their life.

> *"Holding a leadership position in a Christian organization does not make one a spiritual leader. Spiritual leadership is not an occupation: it is a calling. Christian businesspeople, physicians, educators, politicians, and parents—all ought to be spiritual leaders. More and more people in 'secular' occupations are taking their calling as spiritual leaders seriously, and they are impacting the world and extending God's kingdom."*
>
> Henry Blackaby[6]

If serving leaders are going to be fruitful and effective, they need to have a sense of God's calling and purpose. This calling and purpose comes *from* God, not from conjuring up some big mission that we sense will please God. We all are called to participate in God's Eternal Mission. Our work is only important when it is fulfilling God's Kingdom purpose.

God asks us to be about His purposes in whatever context we find ourselves. **Jeremiah 29:11-12** says, *"For I know the plans that I have for you,' declares the LORD, 'plans for welfare and not for calamity to give you a future and a hope. Then you will call upon Me and come and pray to Me, and I will listen to you."* Our understanding of this calling will affect our view of work, money, relationships, and ministry.

The following highlights key thoughts in the three areas of calling.

Overall Call to Ministry

- Calling is three-fold: relational, universal and individual.
- When understood and embraced, our calling should be a primary motivation in our life.
- Our calling becomes an anchor in the midst of a storm. It clarifies our priorities and is the passion that energizes and sustains us daily.
- Calling comes from hearing and listening to God and requires two essential ingredients: emptiness of self (brokenness, humility, death to self) and the willingness to act by faith (obedience).

Relational Calling

- First and foremost, God calls us into a relationship with Himself through Jesus Christ.
- This relationship should be one of a growing intimacy that governs our worldview, values, and behavior.
- Our relational calling (devotion to God) should never be replaced by our universal calling or our individual calling.
- This devotion to Christ (intimacy with Him) is possible only through the means of humility.
- Our relational calling should be developed through the exercise of the spiritual disciplines of prayer, study of God's Word, fellowship, and prayerful solitary reflection.

Universal Calling

- All Christians are called to give their lives away to the lost (evangelism) and to fellow Christians (discipleship). The call to evangelism and discipleship is an absolute, mandatory command of Jesus.
- Our commitment to evangelism and discipleship should flow out of an abundant, intimate relationship with Christ. It is never a substitute for intimacy or a means to develop it.
- This calling is a universal call for every Christian to live out God's purpose and participate in His Kingdom.

Individual Calling

- Our individual calling becomes the context or arena of influence where our intimacy with God grows as we live out His purposes.
- Passion, spiritual gifts, and circumstances play a factor in shaping our individual calling.
- God does not reveal His individual calling if we are not relationally and universally aligned with Him.
- Our calling in terms of individual work will fit into God's purposes and His Kingdom.
- Few are called to full-time vocational Christian work while all are called to be full-time Christians.

Now that we have laid the groundwork for the "what" of calling, we will frame the "how" with some thoughts on the process and examine the specifics of hearing God's call.

PERSPECTIVES ON THE PROCESS

1. God doesn't rush the process (Psalm 46:10).

It is often said God guides and Satan rushes. Watch out when organizations or people put pressure on you to move too fast. Most of the time, speed is not of God. Allow time to pray and get counsel.

2. The need is *not* the call.

Just because there is a **need** does not mean you are called to it. This often is given as the justification of our activity. The need must not be the only reason. Yes, when God calls, there is a need that will be met, but one cannot respond to every need.

3. Stay put until God has clearly called (1 Corinthians 7:17, 21).

God calls us to a vocation including a specific job, location, etc. We are to stay where He has placed us until He clearly prompts us to move. Just because the "grass is greener" or an opportunity arises does not mean it is God's will or His call. This is often the world's approach. If God desires a change for us, it will become very clear as we spend time with Him, and these principles begin to line up.

4. Our calling is an expansion of the ministry or direction we are on.

The calling is compatible with our giftedness. Most of the time, God does not radically take you out of one environment or ministry and place you in another. Although, there are exceptions, our calling often is an extension of the work/ministry where we are functioning.

God does not send us to remote or unknown places unless He puts a desire or burden in our heart to go there.

5. If God is calling us, He will provide (Philippians 4:19; 1 Thessalonians 5:24).

Our calling should not be economically motivated. We must guard against the desire for money. Our priorities must be established and clear because God will test our motives. We need to believe that God will provide for our needs although this may also satisfy our wants.

6. God's call will fulfill His purposes.

When fulfilling God's call, we will be engaged in God's Kingdom purposes. At the heart of God's call are people. We are not called to function as a "lone ranger," independent of people.

7. We hear the call of God only as we are "Intimate with God."

Our vocational calling should flow out of an intimate relationship with God and His command to go make disciples. Intimacy with God is more important than a job. If we are not completely obedient to God, He will not disclose Himself to us (John 14:21).

8. All are called.

God calls every believer to a vocation that becomes the arena where we function as instruments of the gospel. No one profession, such as being pastor, is a higher calling over any other. All legitimate professions are equal in God's eyes. God calls men and women to secular and spiritual functions alike—there is no difference to Him. What do make a difference to God are our motives and how we carry out the work.

SPECIFIC STEPS IN HEARING THE CALL OF GOD

1. Total Surrender.

The clarity of God's calling is heard and understood only after we have died to *our* vision of the calling. If we are not neutral before God (death to self), it is easy to manipulate or rationalize our own desires and give God the credit for it. The call is never a matter of pride or ambition—that is a fast way to disaster.

2. Confirmation from God's Word.

Careful attention needs to be given to God and His Word for the confirmation. This will come naturally. We should never seek to look at specific verses then manipulate them to reinforce a previously held desire. God *will* speak if we will but listen. The call is never outside of a biblical foundation. We hear God by consistently keeping a time of studying and reading the Word of God.

3. Peace.

When God speaks, we will have a peace. We will also experience this peace with our spouse and family. God does not bring confusion or a lack of peace when calling someone. If there is confusion or a lack of peace in the message, you can conclude God is not yet moving (it is either not the time or not His direction). This peace comes from God, though we sometimes attempt to logically explain the details.

4. Confirmation of the call by others. (Proverbs 15:22)

There is wisdom in many counselors. When seeking counsel, make sure you have godly counselors who know you and don't have a vested interest in the outcome. You must be honest as you get counsel, because if you only provide part of the picture, you manipulate the outcome. After receiving counsel, you are ultimately and totally responsible for your decision before God.

5. Pray, Pray, Pray

Much prayer is fundamental to hearing the call of God. In fact, it would be hard to pray too much. Prayer is the real work. God is not playing games with us. He will make His will known. Be diligent and willing to wait for God to answer.

6. Circumstances

Circumstances play a significant role in the direction and timing of God's call. For example, if I sense God's call and it involves a residential move, yet my reasonably priced house does not sell, the message may be one of three things—not the right time, do not make the move (a change of calling), or God did not call. It is when we manipulate the circumstances to force our desired outcome that we are beyond God's call and operating in the flesh.

APPLYING BIBLICAL TRUTH TO OUR LEADERSHIP

Finally it is imperative to express our calling in a written life purpose statement. Writing it out clarifies and creates a grid from which we can prioritize the demands on our time.

9 STEPS TO CONSTRUCTING A LIFE PURPOSE STATEMENT

1. Start from our common purpose as Christians.

Based on our earlier study, what does God desire from us all? Nothing in the rest of your statement can be inconsistent with God's commands.

2. Who are you?

What is your marital status? Family plan? Occupational status? What special skills do you possess?

3. What are your dreams?

God gives us special vision and aspirations.

4. What are your spiritual gifts, skills, abilities, and temperaments?

5. What impressions are you gaining through prayer?

6. What do godly friends say about you that might contribute to your understanding of God's unique purpose for your life?

7. Now take the common purpose and integrate with answers.

- God's universal purpose
- Your unique gifts
- Skills
- Temperament
- Career, family, and personal goals

8. Select Scripture verses God has used in your life to give you direction and purpose.

Choose verses that best characterize His purpose for your life.

9. Begin writing out your purpose statement!

6 DECISIONS THAT WILL IMPACT OUR CALLING

In order to be a servant leader, there are choices and decisions we must make that will put Christ first in our leadership.

1. Individual Posture – Decease or Increase – John 3:30

Character comes from Christ in us, but it is displayed by our choices, the decisions we make. We choose to become a servant—a bond-servant—a role of voluntary service to the master (not under compulsion).

2. Relational Focus – Give or Take – Acts 20:35

Servanthood is not about us, it is about considering the needs of others—helping, caring, building up, etc. Being in community is a daily direction we need to take; we are not designed to live life alone.

3. Transformational Power – Receive or Achieve – John 15:5

The power for serving or leading is not derived from the vessel but from the source that fills the vessel—Christ alive in us. This power is received as we surrender, allowing Christ to manifest Himself through us.

4. Personal Excellence – Weak or Strong – 2 Corinthians 12:9

Your work displays an excellence that reflects and magnifies Christ. The excellence is a product of Christ Himself working through our weaknesses.

5. Eternal Purpose – Kingdom or King – Colossians 1:27-29

Leaders are committed to fulfilling God's Kingdom purposes rather than attempting to be kings of their own realms.

6. Generational Legacy – Today or Tomorrow (Addition or Multiplication) – 2 Timothy 2:2

Leaders give themselves to people, knowing that an investment in others is the only eternal return and reward that lasts. This legacy lasts far beyond their lifetimes.

HOW HUMILITY UNLOCKS THE DOOR TO SERVING

Meet my friend Todd Briggs, pastor in Atlanta, as he tells his story.

"I had met Bruce through a Leadership Round Table, which focused on teaching leadership principles and applying biblical truth to our current situations, contexts, and relationships. I always appreciated Bruce's focus on humility in leadership—kind of a lost art in our Christian context. We regularly dealt with the tension of being a take-charge leader while knowing when to humble yourself before God and those you lead in order to see God truly glorified. So here is what that looks like in real life.

"We had been planting a church in our urban Atlanta neighborhood for three years. We had been in and out of various meeting places. Through the church-planting network I belong to, we entered into a process with an existing church to transfer over the ownership of the facility and the corporate entity of that church to my team and me. The church was dissolving into a messy conflict.

"As the transfer was about to take place, the controlling interests in the previous leadership began to draw the process out. Explaining to people the vision and mission of the church they were visiting was awkward. We had been starting a new congregation with none of the previous church members or leaders attending. We had brought a group with us and God supplied leadership from outside that group ready to start something new. Six months into what was supposed to be a three-month process the outgoing leadership began making overtures that they might like to continue on in leadership with our team. I was very troubled about what kind of disaster I had dragged my family into.

"Bruce and the round-table leaders had been hearing the latest for six months and had been helping me navigate the process. I shared how this failed leadership group was sending signals that they might renege on our agreement. As a group, God led us to see that I needed to place the situation humbly in His hands. Over a few days of prayer, I asked my best prayer warriors to join me. I decided to approach the outgoing leaders and humbly ask that they might honor their word, recognizing that I had no ability, right, or power to make them turn things over.

"They were making a rare appearance at our Sunday service, a first step into handing over of control. Two weeks prior to this, we had agreed on a timetable (this time in writing) to complete the transition in two months; then the overtures about staying had begun. I had planned to approach them after the service. They approached me. They told me that as of that day, two months ahead of schedule, they were going to step down in every capacity, and turn over total control of the facility and corporate entity. They did this by the end of business Monday and the transfer was complete!

"I believe my total assent to the heart of how God wanted me to handle the situation resulted in God making it happen, and He gets all the credit. It's not the latest slick leadership principle that we need; it is biblical truth applied to reality and powered by prayer. That is how we are to lead God's people.

"Since God has given us that facility we have been blessed to share it for as many Kingdom uses as possible: We have a Korean church plant that meets there, we have had local campus ministries and other church plants without buildings use the facility for big events. We have given space to ministries who *serve the homeless and housed mission teams traveling to our city. Humble Leadership is what God is looking for in order to give Him ALL the Glory."*

ONE LEADER PRINCIPLE: Leaders serve as second. Leadership always seeks to humbly serve others ahead of self while living with a clarity on God's purposes.

ONE LEADER PRAYER: (personalize these passages as a prayer to God)

"But it is not this way among you, but whoever wishes to become great among you shall be your servant; and whoever wishes to be first among you shall be slave of all. For even the Son of Man did not come to be served, but to serve, and to give His life a ransom for many" (**Mark 10:43-45**).

"For you were called to freedom, brethren; only do not turn your freedom into an opportunity for the flesh, but through love serve one another" (**Galatians 5:13**).

ENDNOTES

1   *Spiritual Leadership* by Henry Blackaby
2   *Revolution Within* by Dwight Edwards
3   Op. Cit., Blackaby, page 122
4   *Out of Solitude* by Henri Nouwen, pages 36-37
5   *Connecting* by Larry Crabb
6   Op. Cit., Blackaby

Chapter Nine

INFLUENCING TO THE THIRD AND FOURTH GENERATIONS

"The things which you have heard from me...entrust...to faithful men who will be able to teach others also."

Paul the Apostle (2 Timothy 2:2)

INFLUENCING IS ABOUT MOVING PEOPLE TOWARD GOD'S PURPOSES

A successful person who follows the One Leader connects with people and encourages them to adopt the vision—and the goals to reach it—as their own. Leaders earn this kind of influence when they build trust with their followers. Without trust there can be no true leading or following.

TRUST BEGINS WITH BEING CALLED RATHER THAN DRIVEN

Understanding and being true to one's calling is critical to building trust in others, because the calling or cause is bigger than any one person. Operating within one's calling is very different from simply setting goals and driving hard to reach them. This distinction presents a very real tension for Type A leaders who are accustomed to making things happen. In his book, *Ordering Your Private World*, Gordon MacDonald lists some of these symptoms of a driven life.

1. Driven people are most often only gratified by accomplishments and symbols of achievement such as titles, positions, and status. The more stuff on the wall, the better the GPA, the more pages on the resume, the better the driven person feels or at least until they discover someone who has more.

2. Driven people are caught up in the uncontrolled pursuit of expansion. Driven people aren't satisfied with the status quo. In a sense, that's not a bad thing. At the same time, growing a business or a church at all costs can leave lots of casualties in our wake. Driven people tend to like to build their own kingdoms at the expense of others.

3. Driven people often have a limited regard for integrity. Speed and efficiency can lead to cutting corners. Driven people can easily justify making poor ethical choices in order to achieve their ends.

4. Driven people are not likely to bother themselves with the honing of people skills. Driven people tend to use people as a means to an end, rather than seeing them as individuals worthy of attention and love.

5. Driven people tend to be highly competitive. It's not enough to compete. You have to win. Driven people see second place as being the first loser.

6. Driven people often possess a volcanic force of anger. Driven people don't take criticism well because it challenges their perfectionism. Criticism about something we have done gets translated into a value judgment on us as a person. Driven people tend to respond to an attack with overwhelming emotional firepower.

7. Driven people are usually abnormally busy, are averse to play, and usually avoid spiritual worship. I had a mentor once who told me that the biggest thing I'd have to guard against in ministry was the possibility of losing my soul. For ministers who are driven, reading the Bible, prayer, and quiet time can be seen as part of the job. I realize now that when I don't make time for God, I'm the one who suffers.

If you struggle with any of these symptoms of "drivenness," it may be time to do some soul searching. Take time to focus inward and take hold of the fact that God loves us unconditionally. The Christian life is not one of performance and achieving results. It is not one of furious activity in order to gain the acceptance and approval of the Father. God loves you for who you are not for what you do. You must remember: there is nothing that you will do to get God to love you more and there is nothing that you will do that will make God love you less.

It's a constant battle, though. When we get disconnected in our private world, we need to run to the Lord. We can often see the problem in others, but we cannot see it in ourselves. Overcoming drivenness has to be a daily discipline.

Three aspects of influence development that are critical for leaders to understand are:

1. **The chief skill of a leader is to build trust.**
2. **Leaders need to develop skills with an attitude of excellence.**
3. **Develop the next generation of leaders.**

THE CHIEF SKILL OF A LEADER IS TO BUILD TRUST

Building trust in followers is the MOST crucial skill that a leader can develop. People need to see that the leader is walking with the Lord, has a vibrant prayer life and is encouraging others to seek the Lord. People also look for a leader who has both character and competence. The absence of either one of these creates insecurity and distrust among followers. Having already considered the character of a leader in an earlier chapter, we now turn to building trust by developing competence.

Building Trust

I have personally found the following from *The Speed of Trust* by Stephen M. R. Covey to be an excellent tool to help leaders.

Behavior #1: Talk Straight

- Be honest. Tell the truth. Let people know where you stand. Use simple language. Call things what they are. Demonstrate integrity. Don't manipulate people or distort facts. Don't spin the truth. Don't leave false impressions.

Behavior #2: Demonstrate Respect

- Treat everyone with respect. Show kindness in the little things. Behave in ways that demonstrate caring.
- A good leader takes nothing for granted and recognizes the contributions made by everyone on the team.
- Think about specific things you can do to show others you care about them. Call people. Write thank you notes. Give acknowledgment. Send e-mails of concern. Try to do something each day to put a smile on someone's face.
- Never take existing relationships for granted—particularly relationships with loved ones, family, and friends.

Behavior #3: Create Transparency

- Transparency is about being open, real, and genuine and telling the truth in a way that people can verify.
- Disclose relationships, interests, and conflicts ahead of time so that everything is always out in the open.

Behavior #4: Right Wrongs

- Make things right when you're wrong. Apologize quickly. Make restitution where possible. Practice service recoveries. Demonstrate personal humility. Don't cover things up.

Behavior #5: Show Loyalty

- Give credit to others and speak about people as though they were present.
- Go out of your way to give credit freely.

- Make it a rule to never talk about family members in negative ways.

Behavior #6: Deliver Results

- Clarify "results" up front. Make sure you thoroughly understand the expectation.
- Before you make a commitment, make sure it's realistic. To over promise and under deliver will make a withdrawal every time.
- Try to anticipate needs in advance and deliver the requests.
- Establish a track record of results. Get the right things done. Don't over promise and under deliver. Don't make excuses for not delivering.

Behavior #7: Get Better

- In seeking to get better, there are two strategies that are particularly helpful in maximizing your effort: seek feedback, and learn from mistakes (really all experiences).
- Continuously improve. Increase your capabilities. Be a constant learner. Develop feedback systems—both formal and informal. Act on the feedback you receive.

Behavior #8: Confront Reality

- Confronting reality is about taking the tough issues head on. It's about sharing the bad news as well as the good, naming the "elephant in the room," addressing the "sacred cows," and discussing the "undiscussables."
- Address the tough stuff directly. Acknowledge the unsaid. Lead out courageously in conversation.

Behavior #9: Clarify Expectations

- Create shared vision and agreement about what is to be done up front.
- In every interaction—explicitly or implicitly—there are expectations.

- Disclose and reveal expectations. Discuss them. Renegotiate them if needed and possible. Don't assume expectations are clear or shared.
- Clarify expectations both at work and at home.
- Check for clarity by asking a few simple questions:
  » What have you understood from this conversation?
  » As a result of our interaction, what do you see as your next steps?
  » Do you feel that others are clear on expectations?
  » What can we do to make things more clear?

Behavior #10: Practice Accountability

- Hold yourself accountable. When people hold themselves accountable, it encourages others to do the same.
- Hold others accountable. People respond to accountability particularly the performers. They want to be held accountable.
- Take responsibility for results. Be clear on how you'll communicate what you are doing and how others are doing.

Behavior #11: Listen First

- Listen before you speak. Understand. Diagnose. Listen with your ears, your eyes, and heart. Don't assume you know what matters most to others. Don't presume you have all the answers or all the questions.

Behavior #12: Keep Commitments

- Keeping commitments is the quickest way to build trust in any relationship
- Make commitments carefully and then keep them.
- Don't break confidences.

Behavior #13: Extend Trust

- Demonstrate a propensity to trust. Extend trust abundantly to those who have earned your trust. Extend unconditionally to those who are earning your trust.

People trust a leader for whom Christ is the source of life, character, and competence.

LEADERS NEED TO DO ALL THINGS WITH AN ATTITUDE OF EXCELLENCE.

Excellence is important in leadership because of the example it sets and the expectation you have for your followers. If you are a sloppy leader, others will assume they have permission be the same.

In **Colossians 3:23**, Paul teaches, *"Whatever you do, do your work heartily, as for the Lord rather than for men."* This indicates that we work with excellence to glorify God rather than men. It is as if the Lord is our boss.

If a leader fails to pursue excellence, it will undermine his stated values, and his actions will ultimately have a negative reflection on Christ. People will lose faith in the leader and their level of trust will diminish. The work can suffer great loss through the lack of commitment and consistency in pursuing excellence.

Proverbs 22:29 states, *"Do you see a man skilled in his work? He will stand before kings; he will not stand before obscure men."*

Skills contribute significantly to advancement and influence. If we do not perform our functions well, people will not follow as closely, and the results will be less compelling for people to commit and sacrifice.

These quotes stress the importance of attitude.

> *"The longer I live, the more I realize the impact of attitude on life. Attitude, to me, is more important than facts. It is more important than the past, than education, than money, than circumstances, than failure, than successes, than what other people think or say or do. It is more important than appearance, giftedness or skill. It will make or break a company... a church...*

a home. The remarkable thing is we have a choice every day regarding the attitude we will embrace for that day. We cannot change our past... we cannot change the fact that people will act in a certain way. We cannot change the inevitable. The only thing we can do is play on the one string we have, and that is our attitude. I am convinced that life is 10% what happens to me and 90% of how I react to it. And so it is with you... we are in charge of our attitudes."[1]

"It is not the critic who counts: not the man who points out how the strong man stumbles or where the doer of deeds could have done better. The credit belongs to the man who is actually in the arena, whose face is marred by dust and sweat and blood, who strives valiantly, who errs and comes up short again and again, because there is no effort without error or shortcoming, but who knows the great enthusiasms, the great devotions, who spends himself for a worthy cause; who, at the best, knows, in the end, the triumph of high achievement, and who, at the worst, if he fails, at least he fails while daring greatly, so that his place shall never be with those cold and timid souls who knew neither victory nor defeat."[2]

THE IMPACT OF SKILLS

The development of skills can make all the difference between being a good leader and being a great leader. God will use the leader's skills to accomplish His purpose.

In a larger sense, our skills come from God through His gifts of talents and abilities and His building in us the capacity and opportunity to learn, grow, and apply them.

Skills must be seen in this context, or we will sink back into glorifying ourselves by comparing ourselves to others!

A leader with skills is more effective than one who is unskilled, and that directly affects his or her ability to influence others. If a leader is learning and growing in leadership skills, there is less friction, more work is accomplished, and the outside world takes notice. If the skills are not applied, the result is friction and heat between the leader and those being led.

TOOLS IN THE MASTER'S HAND

God has designed every leader to be different. We know that we each have unique gifts, personalities, passions, and experiences. In addition to these qualities, leaders need to add and grow skills (competence) that will greatly enhance their effec-

> *"Much of what passes as leadership, conspicuous position taking without followers or follow through, posturing on various public stages, manipulation without general purpose, authoritarianism—is no more leadership than the behavior of small boys marching in front of the parade, who continue to strut along main street after the procession has turned down a side street to the fairgrounds."*
> **James MacGregor Burns**

tiveness. The complete package of character, calling, and competence allows the leader to be a tool in the Master's hand. Some leaders are surgical instruments, some are megaphones, some are engines, and all have different callings.

Effectiveness and fruitfulness in life and ministry are enhanced by training and developing such skills as vision casting (communication), vision planning, coaching, developing new leaders, and team building.

SUMMARY: RELATIONAL LEADERSHIP

Leadership begins with a spiritual foundation—our relationship with God—and then is lived out on the horizontal plane of human relationships. Our primary relationship must be rooted in our love of Christ. Are you growing and staying connected to Him? Or are you more involved with the task, taking the connection with Christ for granted? If you are not continually seeking and growing in the Lord first, you will find yourself running on fumes. Many leaders overlook this and fall off the path or become easy prey for the enemy.

Following Christ leads to serving others. This is the outward expression of true biblical leadership based on the deep spiritual foundation we have laid. Leaders must always value people ahead of the task; otherwise they will use and manipulate them to accomplish the goals. The Lord is never in this.

As leaders follow and serve well, they naturally progress in influence. So, influence is not the beginning of leadership it is an outgrowth of Christ working through a person and that leader following and serving others. Influence is very important—it is just not first.

As we have seen, influence is a product of trust, excellence and skills. All of these can be honed and improved no matter where you are in your leadership journey.

ONE LEADER PRINCIPLE: Leaders influence to the third and fourth generations. Our influence is built on knowing Him intimately, being a person that He can use, and learning and using skills to be effective.

ONE LEADER PRAYER: (personalize these passages as a prayer to God)

"For this reason also, since the day we heard of it, we have not ceased to pray for you and to ask that you may be filled with the knowledge of His will in all spiritual wisdom and understanding, so that you will walk in a manner worthy of the Lord, to please Him in all respects, bearing fruit in every good work and increasing in the knowledge of God; strengthened with all power, according to His glorious might, for the attaining of all steadfastness and patience; joyously giving thanks to the Father, who has qualified us to share in the inheritance of the saints in Light" (**Colossians 1:9-12**).

"And this I pray, that your love may abound still more and more in real knowledge and all discernment, so that you may approve the things that are excellent, in order to be sincere and blameless until the day of Christ; having been filled with the fruit of righteousness which comes through Jesus Christ, to the glory and praise of God" (**Philippians 1:9-11**).

ENDNOTES

1   Charles R. Swindoll
2   Theodore Roosevelt, "Citizenship in a Republic," Paris, 1910

Chapter Ten

TEAM BUILDING — GO FAST OR GO FAR

*"For where two or three have gathered together in My name,
I am there in their midst"* (Matthew 18:20).

MISSIONAL LEADERSHIP

When leaders possess a firm spiritual foundation, enjoy solid relationships with the Lord and others, and have a good understanding of their roles, they are better prepared to look outward and engage in God's purposes and mission. Missional Leadership is comprised of Team building and having a Kingdom focus.

TEAM BUILDING

It has been said, *"If you want to go fast, go alone; if you want to go far, go with one another."* Initially, life and work are easier when they just involve you because you know where you are, you can control yourself, and you don't have to worry about communicating with and directing others. Yet, any one individual has limited capacity, skills, and talents. In order to multiply our impact, we need to include others—i.e., a team. We will examine three key ideas: Team building, Teamwork, and Coaching, which includes developing the next generation of leaders.

Leaders need to build teams, and every team needs a leader. The concept of working in teams is from the Lord and, in fact, reflects His nature. The following illustration outlines the 4 cornerstones or basic building blocks of Teamwork.

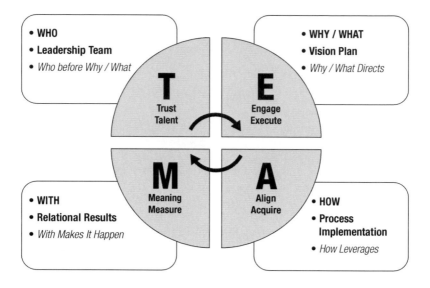

Teams start with people at a *leadership level*. These leaders set the vision and plan for the task. From there the task is given to people at the *team member level* for process development through the leveraging of resources. Finally the team members are empowered to accomplish the task. This teamwork process reflects a balance of people and tasks, yet it starts and ends with people.

All of this teamwork ultimately begins, continues, and ends with Jesus Christ working through people to accomplish His Kingdom purposes.

1. WHO – the leadership engine

Teams always begin with the "who" before the "why" and "what." Any work begins with people who will take a leadership role. This leadership team sets the vision and the plan. This team building process occurs at all levels of an organization.

The Lord calls these people; they are committed to and seek the Lord; they are focused on Christ, the One Leader, living in and through them. Leaders in this quadrant reflect godliness, a servant heart, and maturity.

2. WHY/WHAT – the motivation and direction

The "why/what" begins with God's purposes (evangelism, disciple-ship, multiplication) and our desire to glorify Him above anything else. God is the One who works in and through us to accomplish His purposes.

With this end in mind, the leadership team prays and asks God for His vision and plan. He will reveal His will in His own time and His way. We often get ahead of the Lord if we are not mature, wanting God to rubber stamp our agenda.

3. HOW – the mission in action

The "how" comes down to the processes of the work. What is the model of the work? What systems that necessary? What is success? What must each person or group do to accomplish their part of the vision and plan. This includes the actual work. Systems can include all functions as well as technology, etc. This quadrant includes understanding which resources are required (people, talent, money, machinery, etc.) and acquiring them.

4. WITH – the meaningful relationships and measurable results

The "with" comes down to people working together, being empowered, resolving conflict, delegating, and being accountable. Working through conflict to establish harmonious relationships is critical for a team to be highly effective. People need to be challenged and encouraged to accomplish the goals.

TEAMWORK

Teamwork is crucial for surviving and thriving in today's world, where a high level of collective performance is valued more than individual perfection. Teams simply can produce more than any one individual or a loosely formed group. Teams value individuals, give direction, and bring about a synergy as they link arms together. Teams need leaders that people trust, leaders who will empower them to be responsible.

Teamwork starts with people at the direction level. "Who before What" is a guiding principle.

1. **Begin with Trusted Leadership – leaders are identified and functioning**
   a. Build trust: Trust is about credibility. Credibility boils down into four issues: your integrity, your intent, your capabilities, and your results.
   b. Servant attitude: Have the team members' best interests at heart.

   > *Trusted Leaders exhibit humility, a servant heart, commitment, and a clear value system. This builds trust, inspiration, and passion.*

   "Management is doing things right; leadership is doing the right things." "A leader, any leader, must act for the benefit of others and not for oneself." "No matter the style of the executive, the effective ones also treat people with respect." "... Executives have authority only because they have the trust of the organization. This means that they think of the needs and the opportunities of the organization before they think of their own needs and opportunities. This one may sound simple; it isn't, but it needs to be strictly observed."

   Peter Drucker[1]

The questions the leadership team and/or board should ask include:
- Why are we here? How do we define success?
- How can the board—*this* board—be of most value to the organization?
- What behavior are we settling for?
- What five things we should track as a board?
- Who else? What else?

2. **Gather Talented People – the best people with talent, skills, attitudes, knowledge are on the team**

   a. Embrace the attitude of "everyone makes a difference."

   b. Commit to excellent service. (Do I have the opportunity to do what I do best every day?) (Are my co-workers committed to doing quality work?)

   Talented People bring the needed abilities, expertise, and skills to accomplish the task. They team together as leaders.

The Leadership Team focuses on capturing the Vision and setting the Plan in order to direct the team.

There are no insignificant or ordinary jobs when they're performed by significant and extraordinary people. Ultimately, the more value you create for others, the more value will eventually flow towards you. Knowing you've done your best, independent of the support, acknowledgment, or reward of others, is a key determinant in a fulfilling life.

3. **Capture an Engaging Vision – a compelling future picture of your success**

   a Compelling, clear, concise, memorable = alignment

   b. The vision is tied to the mission and values. (Does the mission/purpose of my company make me feel my job is important?)

   An Engaging Vision brings out the passion of the team, which is the fuel for the mission. Values keep the team on the road.

"Success breeds success." "Nothing succeeds like success."[2] These statements indicate that if you know you can succeed at something, then automatically you'll have the self-confidence

to do it. If you have been successful in the past, you have a better chance at being successful again.

4. Set an Executable Plan – a comprehensive plan with goals, strategies, and action steps

    a. Clear, focused, embraced, opportunity for input

    b. Roles and responsibilities understood (Do I know what is expected of me at work? Do my opinions seem to count?)

An Executable Plan must be comprehensive and detailed so the team can delegate, align, and be empowered.

"A belief that taking action without thinking is the cause of every failure." "What everybody knows is frequently wrong." "Do not simply cling to your past successes; be willing to change, adopt new ideas and continually review all the different segments of business."[3]

Defining Questions/Strategic Direction

Leadership

1. Who is your leadership team?

Vision

2. What is the cause that motivates and compels you?

3. What is the Vision or End Picture?

4. What are the key strategies to achieve the vision?

Mission

5. What is your Mission?

6. Why is this important and significant now?

Values

7. What are the values that will guide you?

Business

    8. What is your business? (the product or service)

    9. Who is the customer and what do they value?

    10.What is your core competence? (what you do best where you are now)

Tactical Action

Implementation

    1. What are your short-term (1 year) and long-term (3-5 year) goals?

    2. What are the plans of action?

    3. How will you do this with excellence?

    4. When should you take action?

Systems

    5. What are the systems and processes needed to keep things on track?

People

    6. What are the resources, people, and technology that are required?

    7. What is the best structure to achieve the vision and plan?

    8. Who will do what?

Results

    9. What are you measuring to assure results and make progress?

    10.To whom are you accountable?

The "How" of a team defines the processes of execution that create alignment and obtain the needed resources.

5. **Work to have Aligned Processes – functions are understood and are being worked on**

   a. The systems and back office are in place to leverage the work.

   b. Technology is being used to accelerate the work. (Do I have the materials and equipment I need to do my work right?)

   Aligned Processes are key to functioning with excellence and producing more with less.

Decentralization and simplification. Drucker discounted the command and control model and asserted that companies work best when they are decentralized. According to Drucker, corporations tend to produce too many products, hire employees they don't need (when a better solution would be outsourcing), and expand into economic sectors that they should avoid. "What's measured improves." "Efficiency is doing better what is already being done." "Follow effective action with quiet reflection. From the quiet reflection will come even more effective action."[4]

6. **Acquire Resources – the tools and finances needed to function**

   a. Leadership provides the resources and tools for success. (Do players have what they need to succeed?) The resources include everything from finances and technology to structure in order to set the roles and responsibilities.

   Acquire Resources is a step that helps leverage the work of the team. It takes assessment and prioritizing because you will never have it all.

The Execution of the team is completed WITH people who work together to achieve results.

7.   **Build Meaningful Relationships – commitment to one another**

a. There is a culture of valuing and serving one another. (Do people at work seem to care about me as a person?) (Does my leader encourage my development?)

Meaningful Relationships are the heart of a team working and achieving its goals. It takes leaders who will empower and trust the team.

Respect of the worker: Drucker believed that employees are assets and not liabilities. He taught that knowledgeable workers are the essential ingredients of the modern economy. Central to this philosophy is the view that people are an organization's most valuable resource and that a manager's job is to prepare and free people to perform.

8.   **Achieve Measurable Results – the team achieves results**

a. Commit to achieving goals with excellence. (Have I received recognition or praise for doing good work?) (Has someone at work talked to me about my progress?) (Have I had the opportunity at work to learn and grow?)

Measurable Results are why a team exists. They get the work done with excellence and timeliness.

"A company's primary responsibility is to serve its customers. Profit is not the primary goal, but rather an essential condition for the company's continued existence."[5]

155

STRATEGIC PLANNING QUESTIONS AND PROCESS

Leadership Team

- Starting point – servant heart, brutally honest
- Character/ model – Agility, authenticity, talent, sustainability
- Process – abandonment, concentration, innovation, risk-taking, analysis

1. **MISSION, VISION, VALUES –**

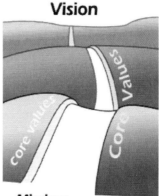

a. Mission – the reason why. What are you trying to achieve? What difference does it make? What will you be remembered for? Fit on a t-shirt (level of communication, understanding and clarity).

b. What is your Vision – positive view of the future. Picture 3-5 years, creates urgency, reinforces passion

c. What are your Values? Non-negotiables, boundaries

d. What is your "critical event"?

e. What is your passion?

2. **CUSTOMER – Who is your customer?**

a. Primary – life who is being changed

b. Who are you satisfying and serving?

c. How are you treating as people?

d. Secondary – everyone who adds to the process, make it happen

3. **VALUE – What does the customer value?**

a. What are their needs, desires, and wants? What is their perception (listen and interview)

b. How does your product /service help and benefit?

4. **RESULTS – What are the results you are working for? 1-year? 3-year?**
   a. How do you measure the results? How do you know you will get there?
   b. How are you doing? What is your business Model?
   c. Be best in class (market), qualitative and quantitative

5. **PLAN – What is your plan?**
   a. Assess the TEAM. Assess the results of the business.
   b. Know the market / competition / comp shop / (react, adapt, or anticipate)
   c. Key Result Areas (necessary components to achieve results
   d. SWOT analysis (Strengths, Weaknesses, Opportunities, Threats) – Set Priorities
      » Product development / manufacturing
      » Leadership – at all levels, empower, communicate, motivate, develop
      » Infrastructure – administration, money, technology, distribution, systems, processes
      » Marketing – communication, advertising, social media, High-tech/high-touch
      » Teams – delegate and empower
      » Quality – process improvement
      » People – building trust, talent, team, competence
      » Build Plan – Strategy (themes), Goals (1 year), Action steps, Set budget
      » Roles / Responsibilities – set and align
      » Accountability; Future – innovation, reinvent

It can be difficult to get even a good team to work well. Patrick Lencioni's book, *The Five Dysfunctions of a Team: A Leadership Fable,* brings this difficulty to light. The principles he describes are:

1. The first dysfunction is an **absence of trust** among team members. Essentially, this stems from their unwillingness to be vulnerable within the group. Team members who are not genuinely open with one another about their mistakes and weaknesses make it impossible to build a foundation for trust.

2. This failure to build trust is damaging because it sets the tone for the second dysfunction: **fear of conflict.** Teams that lack trust are incapable of engaging in unfiltered and passionate debate of ideas. Instead they resort to veiled discussions and guarded comments.

3. A lack of healthy conflict is a problem because it ensures the third dysfunction of a team: **lack of commitment.** Without having aired their opinions in the course of passionate and open debate, team members don't buy in and commit to decisions, though they may feign agreement during meetings.

4. Because of this lack of real commitment and buy-in, team members develop an **avoidance of accountability**, the fourth dysfunction. Without committing to a clear plan of action, even the most focused and driven people often hesitate to call their peers on actions and behaviors that seem counterproductive to the good of the team.

5. Failure to hold one another accountable creates an environment where the fifth dysfunction can thrive. **Inattention to results** occurs when team members put their individual needs (such as ego, career development, or recognition) or even the needs of their divisions above the collective goals of the team.

SUMMARY THOUGHTS ON TEAM BUILDING.

1. Leaders need to build teams and every team needs a leader. **Ecclesiastes 4:9-10**

2. Leadership – *The Right People* who are trusted, talented servants that follow the One Leader and are forward-thinking. **1 Timothy 3:1-10**

3. Priorities – *Doing the Right Things* starting with a big picture and breaking it down to goals and actions. **Ephesians 5:15-16**

4. Systems & Data – *Right* processes and utilizing the right information to deliver healthy financials. **Proverbs 27:23**

5. Execution – *Right Now* is about getting results in a relational environment of valuing people. **Romans 12:9-21**

6. God at Work – *With a Right Foundation* of trusting and allowing God to work and use you as He does it. **Psalm 66:5**

7. Kingdom and Prayer Focus – *And a Right Focus* of always looking to the Lord for His life, strength, and wisdom. **Matthew 13:24-34**

COACH / MENTOR THE NEXT GENERATION

Great leaders will be developing their replacements because their focus is on fulfilling a vision, not maintaining power or position.

> *"Leaders who develop followers grow their organization one person at a time. But leaders who develop leaders multiply their growth because they grow by teams and not individuals. It is the difference between addition and multiplication."*
> **John Maxwell**

For a movement to have a lasting impact in a city or a nation, we need to be intentional about developing leaders. Leadership begins with one person discipling or mentoring another person. This is followed by equipping these disciples with mature teaching and accountability. The goal of our leadership development is for each leader to follow Christ, serve others, and lead teams that will expand the Kingdom in the marketplace.

Who are individual(s) you are developing as future leaders in your sphere(s) of influence? The Bible suggests the value of one man investing in another: *"A little one shall become a thousand, and a small one a strong nation"* **(Isaiah 60:22 KJV)**. WOW! What an impact. This is discipleship lived out.

Multiply future leaders by helping them with a growth plan and in a relational process.

Leaders help others reach a higher level of fruitfulness through trust, participation, and coaching. Leaders are committed to the growth of the individual through hands-on mentoring and training. Use the Leadership Wheel found at the end as a guide for you to develop yourself.

Spiritual Leaders in Ministry, Business, and the Home

Developing leaders is not about teaching facts and verses. It is spiritual reproduction—multiplying the life of Christ in others around the world. Leadership development is a leader's highest priority and the greatest means to multiply their work. This development focuses on building depth and breadth in the leader as they fulfill their calling.

Pray for the growth and development of the future leaders

Paul's prayer for his future leaders as he was investing in them is found in **Ephesians 3:14-19**. It is one of the best prayers that is both an outline and a practical guide to praying for future leaders: *"For this reason I bow my knees before the Father, from whom every family in heaven and on earth derives its name, that He would grant you, according to the riches of His glory, to be strengthened with power through His Spirit in the inner man, so that Christ may dwell in your hearts through faith; and that you, being rooted and grounded in love, may be able to comprehend with all the saints what is the breadth and length and height and depth, and to know the love of Christ which surpasses knowledge, that you may be filled up to all the fullness of God."*

As a leader you will be amazed to see God work as you pray this for those with whom you have influence.

Finally, remember and embrace the words of the Lord Jesus: *"Calling them to Himself, Jesus said to them, 'You know that those who are recognized as rulers of the Gentiles lord it over them; and their great men exercise authority over them. But it is not this way among you, but whoever wishes to become great among you shall be your servant; and whoever wishes to be first among you shall be slave of all. For even the Son of Man did not come to be served, but to serve, and to give His life a ransom for many'"* (**Mark 10:42-45**).

"Go therefore and make disciples of all the nations, baptizing them in the name of the Father and the Son and the Holy Spirit, teaching them to observe all that I commanded you; and lo, I am with you always, even to the end of the age" (**Matthew 28:19-20**).

Equip the next generation of leaders by abandoning your ego, and develop others by drawing out their leadership qualities. That is the method of a true leader. Invest deeply in others. Impart grace to them.

2 Timothy 2:1-2 shows the pattern on investing in one generation to the next—it is a picture of four generations. One needs to be proactive about investing in the next generation. You will need to take some risks and give them a level of authority and responsibility.

Mentoring the next generation will require:

1. Being engaged in their lives, knowing them, and taking time with them—being there over time. It can be messy.
2. Relationships lived out, united in a cause bigger than themselves.
3. Meeting felt needs while continually challenging them to maturity.
4. Modeling and acting with authenticity. Being alongside the younger when the challenges come.
5. Exercising a coaching relationship that helps them grow. Asking more, then telling. Asking them to help you.
6. Empowering them by giving them responsibility and opportunity to grow.

Mentoring can taking many forms and time frames. The key is a heart to heart connection with someone who is further down the path than you. The relationship can be either formal or informal. A mentor-mentee relationship requires work, commitment, and follow-through on both sides if it's going to succeed. So, what aptitudes should you demonstrate to make sure that the mentoring you offer is effective and has lasting value? These are seven key qualities that can help you become an effective mentor.

1. Ability and willingness to communicate what you know
2. Preparedness
3. Approachability, availability, and the ability to listen
4. Honesty with diplomacy
5. Inquisitiveness
6. Objectivity and fairness
7. Compassion and genuineness

Develop the next generation of leaders through coaching

Help others succeed with the **GROW** model. Define **Goals,** know the current **Reality,** discover **Opportunities,** and take action on **What** is to be done. Ask good questions. Hold people accountable. Be intentional.

The Keys to Coaching

1. **Listening:** The first and foremost discipline of a Christian coach is to listen well. Three levels of listening: Internal, Focused, and Global.

2. **Powerful Questions:** the ability to ask insightful or powerful questions. Powerful questions are open-ended questions or probing questions that help the trainee to open up, be vulnerable and to look at the situation from a new perspective.

3. **Goal-setting** is the process of defining where, what, and how you want to proceed in a certain direction for both personal and career opportunities. This process involves two key steps: 1) writing out and crafting a goal, and 2) formulating specific strategies and action steps to reach that goal.

ONE LEADER PRINCIPLE: Leaders leverage best through teamwork. Working together can accomplish God's goals that are far beyond our individual strength and capacity.

ONE LEADER PRAYER: (personalize these passages as a prayer to God)

"Two are better than one because they have a good return for their labor. For if either of them falls, the one will lift up his companion. But woe to the one who falls when there is not another to lift him up. Furthermore, if two lie down together they keep warm, but how can one be warm alone? And if one can overpower him who is alone, two can resist him. A cord of three strands is not quickly torn apart" **(Ecclesiastes 4:9-12).**

"Again I say to you, that if two of you agree on earth about anything that they may ask, it shall be done for them by My Father who is in heaven. 20 For where two or three have gathered together in My name, I am there in their midst" **(Matthew 18:19).**

ENDNOTES

1   Peter Drucker, from "A Class with Drucker"
2   Ibid.
3   Ibid.
4   Ibid.
5   Ibid.

Chapter Eleven

SEEK FIRST THE KINGDOM

*"Seek first the kingdom of God and His righteousness,
and all these things shall be added to you"* (Matthew 6:33).

MAINTAINING A KINGDOM PERSPECTIVE

We are called to always have a Kingdom perspective, yet all too often it's our personal kingdom that we have in view. We tend to focus on our own way, advancing our cause, and have little need for others. Another challenge is confusing activity with end results. Just doing something doesn't mean you are making progress or headed in a Kingdom direction.

As we grow toward spiritual maturity, our perspectives shift greatly. It takes time for us to know and appreciate what the Kingdom is about from God's perspective.

"In the middle of the human story, God introduced the person and Kingdom of His Son as the new way for people to come to know Him. Whoever understands Jesus' mission and opens His inner self to Jesus' forgiveness and presence enters His Kingdom. Kingdom refers to Jesus' ownership of everything that was ever created. We, who were made in God's image and rejected it, have amazingly been given the opportunity to return

to Jesus as Savior and Lord. With this comes a profound inti-macy with the King and a rich relationship with others who are living out a 'yes' to our Royal Master.

"The Kingdom is a spiritual reality in which we participate with heart, soul, and spirit. Our appearance, age, health, education, possessions, race, or shape don't matter. 'Man looks on the outward appearance but the Lord looks at the heart.' There is one king in the Kingdom and many members. The members all have the same importance. No member of the Kingdom stands out by reason of gifts, holiness, or extraordinary adventures be-cause everything that happens in the Kingdom is accomplished by the King Himself. … '"Not by might, nor by power, but by my Spirit," says the Lord Almighty.'"

John Ridgway[1]

Jesus spent much time talking and teaching about the Kingdom of God. As a leader, it is helpful to have an awareness of what God's Kingdom looks like. A number of descriptions of the Kingdom is found in Matthew 13:24-52. The following are simple summaries of these five parables:

1. The Wheat and the Tares

This parable speaks about our relationships and how we live in the Kingdom of God. We are to live among the lost and around those in need of Christ. We are told not to separate ourselves or to live in a "holy huddle." We are to value others and live exemplary lives before them.

2. Mustard Seed

This parable focuses on the idea that size does not matter to God. A little with God is greater than anything in the world. Something that is small and personal to us can be large to God. Kingdom work starts very small but is, in the end, very large when God is at work. The work needs to be seen through God's eyes.

3. Leaven

This parable illustrates how laborers (insiders) in the Kingdom are to penetrate into the community with the Gospel and aroma (appeal) of Christ. It takes just a little "leaven" to create a big change. Like leaven, our work is more internal and spiritual than outward, yet the effects are noticeable over time.

4. Hidden Treasure

This parable helps us see that eternal treasure—spiritual growth and life—is not easily discernible. Kingdom work often brings little recognition in this life. The treasure's value may not be readily seen, but it brings great joy to those who find it. The work of the Kingdom is very valuable, and we are challenged to seek it as we would precious treasure.

5. Merchant Seeking Costly Pearls

This parable tells us that what God values is different than what we—and the world—value. Kingdom work is of great worth, and it should be pursued at whatever cost or sacrifice it may take to obtain it.

These verses expand our view of what is important and what will last. People are eternal and are worth our continual investment because God has paid an infinite price for them. He wants us to labor and to lead in those arenas where He has placed us—to use our skills, talents, and gifts to influence people into a growing relationship with Him.

As we labor daily, we need to do so with a perspective and a focus on God's Kingdom. We must be careful not to confuse activity for true Kingdom work. If our motives and focus are only temporal, we are doing nothing more than stirring up dust.

IT IS ABOUT THE KINGDOM

As we walk with the Lord, we discover that we can't achieve Kingdom results in our own strength. (The branch does not bear fruit through its own effort.) In fact, God doesn't need us, but He chooses to work through us. Our focus needs to be on God's glory and Kingdom, not on gaining recognition for ourselves. We need to be careful what we ask for because the Lord just may give it to us. And, if it is not His best, it can become a hindrance rather than a help.

A Kingdom perspective engenders an outward focus and a servant attitude rather than a selfish, competitive and possessive view. You may have been involved in organizations that are focused on their own end, refusing to help or partner with others in the process. Watch out.

Finally, God calls us to participate in His work by influencing others through excellence and right motives. We are to be stewards of the process, not the closer of the deal.

THE ETERNAL VERSUS THE TEMPORAL

As leaders, to what are we giving our life? At the end of our days, what will we have to show for our labor? These questions should force us to examine our hearts and our priorities. Our end should be eternal and should focus on God's Kingdom purposes. Be careful if your pursuit is temporal. Read from Ken Boa's *Conformed to His Image*:

> *"The temporal and eternal perspectives are competing paradigms of life. We can live as if this world is all there is or we can view our earthly existence as a brief pilgrimage designed to prepare us for eternity. The men and women in Hebrews 11 embraced the latter perspective: 'All these died in faith, without receiving the promises, but having seen them and having welcomed them from a distance, and having confessed that they were strangers and exiles on the earth' (Hebrews 11:13).*
>
> *"People think they want pleasure, recognition, popularity, status, and power, but the pursuit of these things leads, in the final analysis, to emptiness, delusion, and foolishness. God has set eternity in our hearts (Ecclesiastes 3:11), and our deepest desires are fulfillment (love, joy, peace), reality (that which does not fade away), and wisdom (skill in living). The only path to*

this true fulfillment lies in the conscious choice of God's value system over that which is offered by this world. This choice is based on trusting a Person we have not yet seen. 'And though you have not seen Him, you love Him, and though you do not see Him now, but believe in Him, you greatly rejoice with joy inexpressible and full of glory, obtaining as the outcome of your faith the salvation of your souls' (1 Peter 1:8-9)."

Leadership from Christ keeps the eternal in view and is willing to sacrifice the temporal. It may seem costly in the moment, but the outcome is beyond measure and forever.

IMPACTING ETERNITY

As leaders we need to always be engaged in personal evangelism and discipleship, which are the essence of God's purpose. If we lose a connection with helping and influencing others to know Him and grow in Him, we stop growing. We also realize that when we are trying to lead beyond where we are living, we look like a hypocrite and trust is destroyed. Personal ministry creates a need for Christ to work; the focus is not on me but on God's Kingdom. When we begin to focus on the results and the organization, or on our cause, we lose our close connection with Him.

There is One Leader focuses on outcomes that are God honoring and God empowered. The impact of our leadership cannot to be explained by our resources and strategies, but solely upon God showing up and working. Our role is to influence based on an intimate relationship with God and a servant's heart. We are humbled, the world is amazed, and God is glorified. These results will be from the Lord and will further His Kingdom work. Stay connected to God's purposes. These verses give us God's means and ends.

"And we know that God causes all things to work together for good to those who love God, to those who are called according to His purpose" (**Romans 8:28**).

"You are great and powerful, glorious, splendid, and majestic. Every-thing in heaven and earth is yours, and you are king, supreme ruler over all. All riches and wealth come from you; you rule everything by your strength and power; and you are able to make anyone great and strong. Now, our God, we give you thanks, and we praise your glorious name" (**1 Chronicles 29:11-13 GNT**).

PEOPLE ARE ETERNAL

God's desire is that all would come to know and love Him. We are to use all godly means and gifts to labor to this end. Though it is costly, what we will receive will far outweigh the sacrifice. We need to focus on the eternal and influence others to this end.

Leave a Legacy by Developing the Next Generation of Leaders

A final thought for leaders is to always be investing in the next gen-eration of leaders. Great leaders will be developing their replacements because their perspective is for the long-term goal to be accomplished, not to hold on to their positions.

For a movement to have a lasting impact in a city or a nation, we will need to be intentional about developing leaders. Leadership always begins with one person discipling another. This is followed by equipping these disciplers with mature teaching and accountability. The goal of our lead-ership equipping is for each leader to follow the One Leader, serve others, and lead teams that will expand the Kingdom in the marketplace.

Jesus had a paradoxical way of developing leaders. The world tends to look at outward qualities of a leader: looks, charisma, communication skills, motivation techniques, actions, and so forth. Jesus' approach was totally different: first, Christ focused on what was inside the believer. He knew that spiritual transformation is an inside-out process that leads to behavior change. The world, as well as much of Christianity, focuses on developing outward qualities and characteristics without addressing the inner man. In the development of leaders, God offers many promises to encourage our growth. The second way Jesus developed leaders was through experience. It was not just information (another book, seminar, or workshop).

Leadership development is modeled by Paul in his last letter. *"The things which you have heard from me in the presence of many witnesses, entrust these to faithful men who will be able to teach others also"* (**2 Timothy 2:2**). Paul challenges Timothy, a discipler and leader, to multiply the ministry and his leadership by entrusting truth to faithful men who were able to teach others also.

Consider the Legacies of Two Men

The power of a legacy is found in contrasting the lives and legacies of Jonathan Edwards and Max Jukes. The following is a family history of Max Jukes, an atheist who lived in New York during the 19th century. Of Jukes' 560 known descendants:

- 7 were murderers
- 60 became thieves
- 67 reported having syphilis
- 100 were alcoholics
- 50% of the women in his family line became prostitutes
- 300 died prematurely

Now look at the family history of Jonathan Edwards, a brilliant preacher of the Gospel:

- 300 were preachers
- 295 were college graduates
- 100 were missionaries
- 100 were lawyers
- 80 held public office, including 1 Vice President of the United States (Aaron Burr), 13 U.S. senators, 1 state governor, 3 big city mayors and 1 U.S. comptroller

- 75 military officers
- 65 college professors including 13 college presidents
- 56 physicians including 1 dean of a medical school

The power of a legacy can stretch for centuries and touch many generations.

To leave a legacy you must give your life away; you must invest and pour your life into others! Recently, I had the opportunity to go to India with another businessman to share about Christ and His heart for reaching people and expanding God's Kingdom work. The following is an excerpt from my summary of this ministry trip.

"The trip to India was stretching, rewarding, and was very fruitful in God's Kingdom work. Where to begin?

India is incredible—1.2 billion people—75% Hindu, 15% Muslim, 4% Sikh, and 3% Christian. A land of rich spiritual heritage—it is recorded that "doubting Thomas," one of Jesus' disciples, came to southern India in the first century and many trace their roots to that era! The influence of Hinduism is very prevalent, giving a relativistic view to life, people, and spiritual interests. There are unbelievable challenges of crowded and dirty streets, devastating poverty, and a lack of infrastructure. Business and the economy are booming, with an almost 10% annual growth that is creating wealth and a burgeoning middle class of young techies and engineers.

"Rick (my traveling companion) and I saw GOD AT WORK in the lives of many people—Kumara and Annie, owners of a Christian printing and publishing distribution company in Hyderabad, had over 50 people to the training, mostly young men in their 20's who were on fire to take Christ to the marketplace.

Pramod and Sheila—he is a high level executive with a multinational company in Chennai, and both have a deep commitment to reach their peers for Christ. Richard and Annie are overseers of CBMC India and Christ Community Ministries. They live in Madurai and are influencing literally thousands—from businessmen in the boardrooms to destitute women in the streets.

"These were only a few of the key leaders who touched our hearts...We trained these leaders with principles through stories and demonstrating a lifestyle that introduces others to Christ, which, among the Hindu and Muslim faiths, is truly the only way to reach them. We shared our lives, both successes and struggles, gave them tools for equipping, and left them with a process of multiplication.

"Our focus was ministering in the marketplace to reach the future generations, yet we were the ones ministered to by many. Richard Samuel, in particular, shared his passion for the least and the forgotten of India. We visited his ministry among the destitute women and along with his brother, Raymond. We went to their outreach to lower caste factory workers, the school educating young teenagers who have been left behind, and their work in the remote rural villages.

"We experienced the light of Christ shining through so many people—we were deeply touched and blessed. We saw Proverbs 11:25 fulfilled: '...He who waters will himself be watered.' God is at work in His Kingdom through His people."

ONE LEADER PRINCIPLE: Leaders are Kingdom-focused and leave a lasting legacy. They always keep God's Kingdom as the focus rather than themselves.

ONE LEADER PRAYER: (personalize this passage as a prayer to God)

"But seek first His kingdom and His righteousness, and all these things will be added to you" (**Matthew 6:33**).

ENDNOTES

1   John Ridgway, The Navigators, The Kingdom

Section Three

STARTING WELL AND FINISHING WELL

Chapter Twelve

SPARKING A LEADERSHIP REVOLUTION

HOW WE FINISH IS DETERMINED BY WHERE WE START

We all want to finish well and echo the apostle Paul, *"I have fought the good fight, I have finished the course, I have kept the faith"* (**2 Timothy 4:7**). We want to be pleasing to God and hear, *"Well done, good and faithful servant"* (**Matthew 25:21**). This desire to finish well is why we have leaders, teams, and organizations and why we seek to accomplish a greater good for others by extending God's kingdom.

As we have stated, God is very interested in *how* we serve—the process—because He is solely in charge of the results. The challenge is that we can be tempted to justify using the wrong means to obtain a "good" end; ultimately, doing that will lead us away from God's intended goal, not toward it.

Furthermore, leaders must have the right starting point, which is Christ and Christ alone. When we define leadership as "influence" or "character," we often overlook the fact that these activities can be done in the *flesh* (our own strength).

If we start with influence, our leadership can look no different than the world's, with its emphasis on skills, talents, charisma, and appearance. These all can be developed and used apart from Christ leading through us. In fact, the work can be done without integrity or valuing people. This type of influence honors man more than it honors God.

Likewise, if character is the starting point of leadership, the source behind this character can be either human-driven or Christ-driven. Jim Collins in his book, *Good to Great*,[1] talks about Level 5 Leaders who exhibit humility and possess a servant attitude. Yet, even in his examples, there is no thought that these leaders are Christians who let Christ work through them.

Character can be built in our own strength. We can do good, be honest, and help others and not know Christ. But true, godly character comes only from Christ. The world and the flesh can exercise leadership that looks good and accomplishes good things. The problem is that it will have no eternal consequence or outcome. It will be wood, hay, and stubble (see 1 Corinthians 3:10-15).

In the **Christ Life Leadership** model, Christ is the beginning, the means, and the end. This principle is underscored by Paul in **Romans 11:36**, *"For from Him and through Him and to Him are all things. To Him be the glory forever. Amen."*

So, as we launch out in our leadership growth and application, we must keep this principle before us constantly.

The Lord will empower us to follow this **Christ Life Leadership** model and to be His agents of change in this fallen world. We'll become a different kind of leader. This process will be a catalyst for world impact and ignite a leadership revolution.

Lead-er-ship *n.* – The function of one who goes before or with to show the way; to guide or influence in direction, cause, or action.

Rev-o-lu-tion *n.* – A radical, complete, and pervasive change in a society or system.

A "leadership revolution" can be defined as a radical and complete change in how one guides or influences. Biblical Christian leadership is nothing more than the overflow of the indwelling Christ working and leading through us.

To make the great discovery of Christ as the one true Leader and yet hold that light under a bushel is self-serving. The love of Christ should compel us to let that light shine as we go into all the world and make disciples. Armed with God's unlimited power and resources, we should be spawning movements of the Gospel in our own Jerusalem, Judea and Samaria, and then on to the ends of the earth (see Acts 1:8).

From this place of Christ living in us, we are made whole. We have His assurance that we are never alone, and through His life we can powerfully minister His grace to a world in great need!

The vision of this teaching is nothing less than a total transformation of how we lead in the arenas of influence where the Lord has placed us. It will challenge us to disciple and mentor future leaders from a new perspective.

Our desire is to start a revolution in our homes, businesses, ministries, communities, and the nations of the world. We need to radically change how we approach leadership and how we function as leaders. The change takes place on a number of levels. Let us make a brief review of the principles found in the **Christ Life Leadership** model.

THE SOURCE OF LEADERSHIP – JESUS CHRIST

There is One Leader and you are not it! This is the primary and fundamental difference between this teaching on leadership and that of the world. Just as we cannot live the Christian life apart from Christ, neither can we lead apart from Him. He is the Leader in us and is the one who leads through us. He is the hand and we are the gloves. The implications of this shift our focus of leadership from the end results to the starting source—Christ. To finish well, we must start well. If we lead with *our* end in mind, we will miss God's will. If we lead with our capacity and resources, we will burn out or go off track.

Practically, we must move from the "how" of leadership to the "who" of being a leader. With Christ as the source of our leadership, God meets our deepest needs for approval, acceptance, and relationships. We come to know that we are never alone, and from this truth we touch the greatest needs of others.

The Process of Leadership

The process shifts from our incessant love affair with leadership as influence to the more complete three-part process: Following, Serving, and then Influencing. It includes the who, the what, and the how. Leadership development is an inside-out growth process.

The Heart of a Leader: Following

The heart of a leader is found in *following* Christ and living in intimate relationship with Him. We shift our attention from trying to "lead like Jesus" (imitation) to the "life" of Christ leading through us (incarnation). Leadership is not about trying harder or just bringing more assets to the table; rather, leadership begins with our intimacy with Him, our new identity in Christ, and His indwelling power. Leadership is all about working "from" Him and not trying to do things "for" Him. The biblical picture is that of the vine and the branches in **John 15:5** where Jesus says, *"apart from Me you can do nothing."*

The Focus of a Leader: Serving

The next part of the revolution is the focus of our leadership, "how" we function in our roles. *Serving* others becomes central. Leadership is relational in nature. Leaders serve people rather than trying to serve themselves, keep their positions, or be totally consumed with accomplishing their tasks. The shift occurs when we focus on loving God, culminating in obedience (see John 14:21). We are moving from doing to being. In others words, our motives and intents are just as important as the outcomes. We will be judged and rewarded on both. Our world embraces the look and the image of an endeavor; God pays attention to a right heart and the right reason.

The Results of a Leader: Influencing

Leadership outcomes shift from being consumed with the building of organizations and institutions to being a catalyst for a movement of God. *Influencing* is about the Kingdom, not about our skills and talents.

These are simply means to His end. Change centers on giving away power (empowerment) rather than holding on to and wielding power. Our results should be consumed with glorifying God, doing His will, and propagating His Kingdom; anything less wrongly shines the light on us.

APPROPRIATING CHRIST AS LEADER IN OUR LIVES

For Christ to be alive in us and be real in our everyday life, we must know Him intimately, take hold of who we are in Him, and allow Him to be released through us in our actions. This process is called "appropriating" Christ, which is the connection between Following and Serving.

Practically speaking, "appropriating" Christ starts with a growing intimacy that we have outlined in detail (seeking Him through prayer, the Word, worship, and so forth). Layered upon this is the belief—and resulting behavior—of our secure identity in Christ. This is characterized by a growth process evidenced by glorifying God and not ourselves, allowing God to meet our needs on His timetable and in His ways, and knowing that we are significant because of what Christ has done and is doing rather than any self-effort to prove our spirituality.

Appropriating Christ is an ongoing process of dying to self, surrender, obedience, gratitude, and putting others ahead of ourselves.

We recognize that obedience encompasses more than behavior; it includes motives, attitudes, and a right process. This leads us to be thankful in everything. Furthermore, all of this must not be self-serving but in service of others. This helps others know Christ and walk with Him, resulting in our long-term participation in God's Kingdom work and coming full circle to glorify God.

These truths emerge from the idea that God does not exist for us, but we exist for Him. We fit into His Kingdom purpose. God only asks from us what He has already placed in us. Our lives become a well of living water being released through us. *Jesus stood and cried out, saying, "If anyone is thirsty, let him come to Me and drink. He who believes in Me, as the Scrip-*

ture said, 'From his innermost being will flow rivers of living water'" (**John 7:37-38**).

LEADERS FINISH WELL

Finally, leaders are committed to finishing their lives well. They put their hand to endeavors that extend God's Kingdom. The following are nine keys to finishing well. It is not easy, but we can finish well—with God's help—if we are intentional about it.

1. A white-hot passion and a growing, intimate relationship with the Lord—Christ as life, spiritual disciplines, ministry to God, worship, and praise.
2. A humble spirit—know your strengths and weaknesses.
3. Healthy relationships with spouse and family—resolving conflict, emotions, care.
4. Being a part of a community with other humble, broken believers—it could be a church or other committed relationship.
5. A simple lifestyle—be debt free, not entangled or in slavery to money, practice contentment, practice enjoyment.
6. A clear sense of purpose and calling—priorities, margin.
7. Engage in a ministry of discipleship and evangelism.
8. Continue to be a learner—read, learn new things, involve your mind and heart.
9. Keep focused on God's Kingdom—God at work, spiritual battles, the Second Coming, eternal vs. temporal, biblical perspective on life.

FINAL APPLICATION: Take inventory of your leadership on the next page with The Leadership Success Wheel. Begin to make notes in areas where you desire progress, and set out a plan to take action. Share it with a friend and have them hold you accountable.

THE LEADERSHIP SUCCESS WHEEL

Rate your satisfaction level on a scale of 1 to 10 for each of the categories in the Leadership Success Wheel (circle a number on the wheel, or simply write the number in the table below the graphic; 10 being the highest and 1 the lowest). Connect the numbers to see where any imbalance occurs.

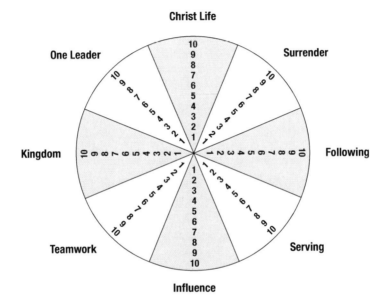

Write In Your Current Level (1=low; 0=high)	Description of each category in the Leadership Success Wheel
	Christ Life – Leadership begins with Christ leading in and through you. We don't lead like Jesus; He leads through us. It is His life in us that is critical.

	Surrender – Leaders have experienced a spiritual sense of surrendering and allowing Christ to fully rule and reign in them. They know brokenness that produces character.
	Following – Leaders are growing in a deepening intimacy with Christ, have know their true identity of being in Christ and are experiencing the power of Christ's indwelling Spirit.
	Serving – Leaders serve people. They display humility and an exhibit an attitude of serving others to fulfill God's purposes.
	Influence – Leaders are growing in influencing other through building trust, working with excellence and growing in learning leadership skills.
	Teamwork – Leaders and teams are critical for success. The leader needs a team and the team needs a leader. Leading a team greatly leverages the work.
	Kingdom – A leader focuses on God's Kingdom purpose while engaging in their sphere of influence and their role. Leaders are stewards of the "process" and the Lord produces the fruit.
	One Leader – Growing and maturing as a leader while seeing Christ bear much fruit in and through you.

Now, please answer the following questions.

1. When you steward the process, what will be different about your business, ministry, or personal life? (Please be specific with respect to impact on leadership, business success, influence, time, schedule, quality of life, self-esteem, income, sense of purpose, fulfilling your calling, and relationships.)

2. What is the most important thing you'd like to accomplish as a result of this study?

3. On a scale of 1 to 10, how committed are you to making this happen?

Movements begin with the radical Christ indwelling passionate leaders. These leaders have a transcendent Kingdom vision and are committed to serving others with humility and creating healthy relationships. They innovate and mobilize in response to the current need.

Let the Leadership Revolution Begin!

ONE LEADER PRINCIPLE: The Lord is searching for those steward leaders whom He can work through to bring about a spiritual revolution beginning with every individual to the every nation on earth.

ONE LEADER PRAYER: (personalize this passage as a prayer to God)
"Jesus came up and spoke to them, saying, 'All authority has been given to Me in heaven and on earth. Go therefore and make disciples of all the nations, baptizing them in the name of the Father and the Son and the Holy Spirit, 20 teaching them to observe all that I commanded you; and lo, I am with you always, even to the end of the age'" (**Matthew 28:18-20**).

ENDNOTES

1   *Good to Great* by Jim Collins, HarperBusiness, 2001

Chapter Thirteen

THERE IS ONE LEADER AND YOU ARE ... NOT IT! REVIEW

PRINCIPLES OF LEADING FROM CHRIST

God uses leaders who are available vessels, He doesn't need our best effort in our own strength. Spiritual leadership is the leadership Christ lived then... and lives now, by Him, in you.

Foundational Truth: There is One Leader and You are not it!

Christ is the one, true Leader (Matthew 23:10, Matthew 28:18), and He has been given all authority (Matthew 28:18). Christ's model of leadership was an abiding relationship with the Father (John 14:10), and He repeatedly taught that He did nothing on His own initiative; it was God the Father working through Him. True leadership shifts the Source of power from ourselves to Him.

APPLICATION: *Christ is the Leader working through us when we allow God to be in control and be in charge of the results. We are stewards of the process. We participate in God's work; we don't contribute to it. God is the origin of His own activity and source of His own power.*

Functional Role: We all function in roles of leadership. Christ works through our uniqueness to serve others and glorify His Kingdom.

Our leadership begins as we follow Him (Matthew 4:19), serve others (Luke 22:26), and then influence others (Matthew 28:19-20) to God's Kingdom purposes. We join Christ in leading when we allow Him to be the hand and we fulfill the role and responsibility of the glove. It is a process of knowing (Follow), being (Serve), and doing (Influence). God uses us in His plan by our walk, our character, our valuing others, and applying skills.

APPLICATION: *We need to step back from focusing on influence and follow first, serve second, and then we can influence with God's Kingdom in perspective.*

Growth Process: Transformation in leadership is from the inside out.

Our development begins with having a godly worldview (Christ's life in me), embracing God's values (character, community, calling), and then focuses on behavior (skills, teamwork). Leadership is a process of inner transformation. Focusing first on your worldview shapes your values,

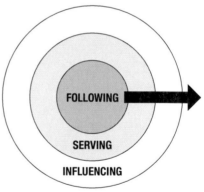

and your values, in turn, shape your behavior. Growth is a lifelong pursuit, with its challenges and rewards.

APPLICATION: *We mature and grow by obedience and faith.*

KEY PRINCIPLE:

LEADERSHIP IS RECEIVED, NOT ACHIEVED

RECEIVED	ACHIEVED
Christ is most important	Cause is most important
Focus on being available	Focus on power
Focus on being used by God	Focus on top position
Humility	Effort
Steward of the process	Focus primarily on results
Working from Christ	Working for Christ

Your leadership is limited, yet it becomes unlimited when Christ is the beginning, means, and end.

Become a leader through whom God works. We lead from Christ, not for Him. God uses leaders who are available. He doesn't need our effort in our strength. Spiritual leadership is the leadership Christ lived then and lives now, by Him, in you.

SEVEN FOUNDATIONAL PRINCIPLES THAT WILL REVOLUTIONIZE YOUR LEADERSHIP

Leadership Development is inside out: *Spiritual, Relational, Missional.*

SPIRITUAL –
1. There is One Leader and You are ... Not It!
2. Leadership is released through Brokenness and Surrender.

RELATIONAL –
3. Leadership is formed by Following First.
4. Leadership is modeled by Serving as Second.
5. Leadership is expanded by Influencing to the Third and Fourth Generations.

MISSIONAL –

6.   Leadership is leveraged through Teamwork.

7.   Leadership is focused on God's Kingdom and leaves a Lasting Legacy.

SPIRITUAL – The following principles are SPIRITUAL. Our worldview follows Christ as our life and leader. As available vessels, we accept our role as faith-filled leaders (Hebrews 11:6).

1.   The SOURCE: There is One Leader and You are … Not It!

Christ is the Source of our leadership (Matthew 23:10). He lives in us and He leads through us (Galatians 2:20) to triumph (2 Corinthians 2:14).

SOURCE: Our leadership begins by receiving Christ as our life and allowing Him to lead through us. We must know that God is in control and author of the results. We are stewards of His life in us, His people, and the process. We participate in God's work, we don't add to it. We are the gloves. He is the hand (the power). Christ has the authority and position of Leader; we function in the role of leadership for our life, family, business, and ministry.

"If Jesus provides the model for spiritual leadership, then the key is not for leaders to develop visions. The key is to obey and to preserve everything the Father reveals to them of His will. Ultimately, the Father is the leader."

Henry Blackaby[1]

RELATIONSHIP: Christ did nothing on His own initiative. His leadership was derived from a relationship with the Father (John 14:10). Our leadership is received from a relationship.

LIFE: Our focus is not to lead "like" Jesus, rather it is to receive His "life" and let Him lead through us. In Him we will have the victory (John 10:10, Philippians 1:21, Colossians 3:3).

ATTITUDES:

Thankful – Be thankful and grateful in every circumstance. It is the simplest expression of faith and prayer. 1 Thessalonians 5:18 and Philippians 4:6-7 call us to be thankful in everything. We can always be thankful that God is in charge and has our best interests at heart.

Grace – The life of Christ is summed up by grace that is given to us. We are stewards of this grace toward others (1 Peter 4:10), especially with difficult people (2 Timothy 2:1).

ACTIONS:

Glorify God – Give praise, honor, and worship to God in all things. To live is Christ (Philippians 1:21). Do this by looking and recognizing that God is working in all things (Psalms 66:5). Be a light by serving (Matthew 5:16).

Stewardship – We have the responsibility of managing or stewarding the process through our motives, attitudes, and handling of people (1 Corinthians 4:2). Love what God loves (Matthew 25:40). Have right priorities. Quit controlling.

2. **The POWER: Leadership is released through Brokenness and Surrender.**
"I must decrease that He might increase" (**John 3:30**).

BROKENNESS: God brings us to the end our resources by pain and trial.

SURRENDER: This is the choice we make to give up. We die to self and thus release His life and leadership. The power of Christ is manifest in weakness (2 Corinthians 12:9). Out of death comes life and fruit (John 12:24).

SACRIFICE: Leadership is costly. Leaders give up personal agendas to give themselves to others (Matthew 16:25).

ATTITUDES:

Humility – Give up your agenda and what you want to do FOR God. Be a learner from others. Put others ahead of yourself (James 4:6-7). Give credit; don't take it. Let go of striving (Psalm 46:10).

Patience – Listen and learn before telling. Use self-control. Wait upon the Lord. Quit being busy. Seek rest. Be unhurried (Matthew 11:28-30).

ACTIONS:

Accountability – Submit to others. Have a group that will tell you the truth and say no. Seek godly counsel of others who will encourage and correct. Find a safe place (Proverbs 15:22). Be real.

Dying to Self – Examine your flesh patterns, confess them, and turn away. Put others' interests ahead of your own (Philippians 2:3-7).

RELATIONAL – The following principles are RELATIONAL. Our role as relational leaders grows when we Follow, Serve, and Influence. People are more important than the task. Our being frames our values, and LOVE is the foundation for all relationships (1 Corinthians 13, Matthew 22:37-39).

3. The FOUNDATION: Leadership is formed by Following First.

Leadership begins by following (Luke 9:23) in a relationship with Christ. It does not begin with us. Following is walking by faith. It is not competing, comparing, counting, or controlling.

INTIMACY: Love brings wholeness (received not achieved).

Leadership flows from a love relationship we receive from the Lord and is ceaseless, causeless, and measureless. Love is realized as Christ lives in us; it is not from a position or behavior. Intimacy with Him connects us to His Life. Christ is the vine. We are the branches, and apart from Him we can do nothing (John 15:5). We are pleasing to God. By receiving His life and love, we are whole and healed. Our first ministry is to God (love) not for God (mission).

IDENTITY: Security, significance, and satisfaction (from not for)

God has made us new creations "in Christ." We lead from this new identity by faith. Our identity in Christ gives us security, significance, and satisfaction. We have every spiritual blessing in Him (Ephesians 1:3). "In Christ" our needs are met; we are accepted, complete, fully loved, and secure.

INDWELLING: He is power and wisdom (Christ-Life not Christ-Like).

Christ living in us provides us with eternal life (Colossians 1:27). The power of Christ is beyond what we can ask, think, or do. His indwelling life gives us power, life, peace, and wisdom, so that He is our strength and we function from calm not anxiety (Colossians 2:6-7). It is "being" before "doing."

ATTITUDES:

Wholeness – You are complete in Christ (Colossians 2:10). He is growing you and healing you of pain and your past in order for Christ to fully flow through you, enabling you to give yourself away to others.

Confidence – By knowing who you are in Christ, and the infinite worth and value you are in God's eyes, your belief in yourself grows tremendously. Do not let the world define who you are. His divine power has granted everything that pertains to life and godliness (2 Peter 1:3).

ACTIONS:

Spiritual Disciplines – Develop specific patterns of prayer and knowing God's Word in order to follow. In particular have a periodic half day of prayer, and be continually reading, studying, and applying the Bible (1 Thessalonians 5:17, Colossians 3:16).

Decision-making – Learn how to listen to the Lord, follow Him, and walk in His will. This is the framework to make sound decisions and take action (Daniel 11:32). God will direct each of us if we are neutral and only desire to do His will. This will require obedience and perseverance.

4. The HEART: Leadership is modeled by Serving as Second.

Christ led by serving (Mark 10:45). Leadership must focus on serving Christ and others in humility. Serving begins with an inward transformation and then works outward.

CHARACTER: Models humility, integrity, obedience, respect, and maturity. Christ's leadership is displayed in and through us by dying to self, our obedience, and maturity. We embrace our difficulties and weakness so His power is evident. Struggles mold us and form humility and maturity, which build bridges of trust (James 1:2-4). Character is integrity, grace, and respect (1 Timothy 3:1-7, Titus 1:5-10). We are to keep growing towards maturity.

COMMUNITY: Leadership values and serves others. Leadership serves people, not tasks (Luke 22:26). Greater love has no one than this: to lay down one's life for one's friends (John 15:13). Serving values people and creates a community that brings many gifts and expressions of the Spirit. We need each other in our weaknesses and strengths. Leadership creates environments of safety and trust while diligently resolving differences and conflicts.

CALLING: Leadership lives and engages in God's purposes. We are to know the hope of our calling (Ephesians 1:18). Purpose gives our leadership direction, priorities, and hope. We are created for good works to walk in them (Ephesians 2:10). It is not defined by a position or organization. It comes from Him and is lived where He places us by pursuing the eternal over the temporal. Goals do not equal outcome; priorities always equal outcome. Write out your life purpose (Colossians 1:28-29). "He is no fool to give up what we can not keep to gain what he cannot lose." Jim Elliot

ATTITUDES:

Encourage – We are to encourage and build up others. We grow when we disciple and help others grow. Serving begins by putting the interests of others first (Philippians 2:3-4) and our needs and personal interests second (1 Thessalonians 5:11).

Kindness – Affirm others with good deeds and notes (1 Corinthians 13:4).

ACTIONS:

Conflict resolution – Work in unity and peace. Resolve differences. Listen in order to understand. Do not try to fix others. Empty self of agendas, let go of controlling. Restore broken relationships. Exercise confession, forgiveness, and comfort in order to meet needs and heal hurts. Be the first to forgive to release its grip (Galatians 6:1-2).

Life Purpose – Align yourself with God's universal purpose of evangelism and discipleship to be a person who is fulfilling their life purpose. Write it out and begin to live it. Let it guide your priorities (Jeremiah 29:11-12).

5. **The PROCESS: Leadership is expanded by Influencing to the Third and Fourth Generations.**

Leadership keeps God's Kingdom in perspective and this defines our outward relationships (2 Timothy 2:2). True leaders grow their skills.

TRUST: Influence begins with trust and faithfulness. People trust when you have Christ, display godly character and demonstrate competence. Build trust with integrity, honesty, listening, caring, and admitting fault (1 Corinthians 4:2).

EXCELLENCE: We are to reflect Christ in all we do. Do your very best rather than trying to be the best. Reflect Christ by having an attitude of excellence and serving the Lord. Others will follow. Be pleasing in all respects. Always do the next, best, right thing (Colossians 3:23).

SKILLS: Leadership is skilled in investing in and guiding others. We influence as we improve skills to be more competent, effective, and fruitful. We work with excellence to the Lord (Proverbs 22:29). The goal is to glorify God and help people find Christ. We all are to grow in winning the lost and making disciples. Skills of team building, vision planning, coaching, delegating, decision-making are very important. Be adaptable. Form will follow function.

ATTITUDES:

Improvement – Seek to grow, change, and innovate in your work. Be the change you want to see. Don't accept the status quo (Luke 10:42).

Diligence – Work hard; always do your best (Proverbs 10:4).

ACTIONS:

Clear communication – Effectiveness and fruitfulness begin with listening, understanding, and clarifying expectations. It is a two-way street.

Empowerment – Give away your positional power. Delegate in order to grow others. Do not keep yourself at the center of all decisions and actions. Help others be successful and give them more responsibility (Exodus 18:17-23).

MISSIONAL – The following principles are MISSIONAL. Taking impactful steps of faith for God's Kingdom frames our actions and behavior. HOPE compels us to reach people and the world (1 Timothy 3:17-18, 1 Peter 3:15).

6. **The MULTIPLICATION: Leadership is leveraged through Teamwork.**

"Two are better than one for they have a good return for their work" (**Ecclesiastes 4:9**).

TEAM: Leadership leverages by teaming and empowering.

1. Build your leadership team with talented people and trustworthy character.
2. Seek God's vision, His plan, and strategy.
3. Define the processes and how to implement the plan.
4. Develop healthy relationships to obtain measurable results.

TEAMWORK: Building teams takes hard work. The process of building teams is central to accomplishing goals. Teams are all about relationships and empowering people. Trust is the beginning step of building a team. Get the right people on the bus and build them up. Help them know their roles and responsibilities. Leadership resolves differences and maintains healthy communication in their team. Leadership adapts according to the needs.

COACH: Help others succeed with the GROW model. Define Goals, know the current Reality, discover Opportunities, and take action on the What is to be done. Ask good questions, hold people accountable.

ATTITUDES:

Value People – Seek their ideas and insight. Be alongside and adapt your style to direct, mentor, coach, or send based on needs (Philippians 2:5-8).

Respect – Believe the best about people.

ACTIONS:

Vision planning – Teams need to know God's vision and plan. This needs to be comprehensive yet inspiring and compelling.

Strategy – Define the priorities and action items with concrete action steps.

7. The GOAL: Leadership is focused on God's Kingdom and leaves a Lasting Legacy.

Leadership chooses the eternal over the temporal gain (Matthew 6:19-20). They give their life to people (Isaiah 54:2-3).

KINGDOM: Leadership partners with God in His purposes. We seek God's Kingdom first and glorify Him (Matthew 6:33).

ETERNITY: Kingdom keeps the eternal in perspective; it is where we will have true reward. Leadership doesn't focus on building organizations that are great; these are only a means to God's end, which is to help people know Him and to bring Him glory (Isaiah 43:4, 7). Without Christ as Life and Leader, we are the limited; yet, leadership impact becomes unlimited when Christ is the beginning, the means, and the end.

MAKE DISCIPLES: Be engaged in Christ's Great Commission. We must be committed to making disciples of all nations (Matthew 28:19-20). Invest spiritually in others. Develop a vision for the world. Be engaged in God's Kingdom, not building your own (Isaiah 58:10).

Develop the next generation and leave a legacy. Do this by personal involvement and guidance. Go deep with a few. Have an attitude of investing and building up others (Galatians 4:19). Leadership doesn't compete, compare, count, and control, but serves, invests, and leaves a legacy (1 Thessalonians 2:8).

ATTITUDES:

Generosity – Be generous by giving to others. Do more than what is expected. You will reap what you sow. Generosity starts with being content and invests in God's Kingdom work. Be involved with the least and the last.

Give – Give your time, talent, treasure, relationships, and grace. You will be rewarded in eternity (2 Corinthians 9:6-8).

"People do not choose to become spiritual leaders. Spiritual leadership flows out of a person's vibrant, intimate relationship with God."

Henry Blackaby[2]

ACTIONS:

Partner with others – Develop working relationships with other teams and organizations. Don't be isolated or try to do everything yourself (2 Timothy 1:8). Help and serve others.

Collaborate – Finds ways to network.

The foundational principles presented in this book are His principles, and He is the source of all leadership wisdom. Follow the One Leader, Jesus Christ, and you'll always be a success.

ENDNOTES

1   *Spiritual Leadership* by Henry Blackaby
2   Ibid.

EPILOGUE

God says, *"It is too small a thing that You should be My Servant to raise up the tribes of Jacob and to restore the preserved ones of Israel; I will also make You a light of the nations so that My salvation may reach to the end of the earth"* (**Isaiah 49:6**).

Leadership Revolution is a ministry singularly focused on leveraging leaders for a Kingdom impact. The difference is that Christ is the beginning, means, and end of His activities. God does not need us to do His work for Him. We are participating in His Great Commission. The work God is interested in is His work through us and not our efforts on His behalf.

Leadership Revolution begins with the truth that Jesus Christ is the only Leader—*"Do not be called leaders; for One is your Leader, that is, Christ"* (**Matthew 23:10**). Christ is saying that it is He who lives and leads through a person. Jesus also taught His disciples, *"I do not speak on my own initiative, but the Father abiding in Me does His work"* (**John 14:10**). Jesus did not speak or lead on His own. His way of leadership was to allow His Father Who was abiding in Him to provide the spiritual resources to do the work. God wants us to lead from our resources of being "in Christ" and to exercise power and authority from this relationship with Jesus.

The ministry of **Leadership Revolution** provides leaders from businesses and ministries access to a dynamic growth process that includes spiritual formation, coaching, strategic planning, and team building.

Mission: To develop and multiply servant leaders who live as Christ and mobilize others to reach their world.

Vision: To train and equip leaders in cities and nations who will multiply future leaders and leverage their influence in their businesses and ministries.

Value Added: The spiritual formation of **Leadership Revolution** centers on Christ's Life, and He is literally working through us. God at work is infinitely better than our best work for Him. The spiritual formation unleashes God's work and ways through our leadership. The relational processes of **Leadership Revolution** allow us to experience truth and see lasting life change. Men and women are being taught how to release the power of Christ through their life allowing Christ to be the Leader.

"CHRIST AS THE ONE LEADER" is a message that is transforming leaders, families, and businesses around the world! This is the uniqueness of Leadership Revolution, and it is what the Lord is using to impact so many.

SMALL GROUP DISCUSSION QUESTIONS

CHAPTER ONE
The Cry of the Heart – A World in Need

1. What is your reaction to the statistics on leadership?

2. What are the greatest challenges you face as a leader?

3. Take some time to reflect on what makes a leader.

4. What do you hope to gain from this book?

CHAPTER TWO
The 10 Myths of Spiritual Leadership

1. What is your reaction to this assessment?

2. How did you do?

3. Which answer did you struggle with the most?

CHAPTER THREE
An Eternal Life Lived in a Temporal World

1. How is leadership lived out in the temporal arena with an eternal perspective?

2. Comment on the truths that frame Christ Life Leadership.

3. How do values affect our leadership? Describe your specific values as a leader.

4. Review the benefits of our eternal life; how will this help your leadership?

_____

_____

_____

_____

_____

5. Why is embracing leadership as a stewardship important?

_____

_____

_____

_____

6. How would giving up control affect your leadership?

_____

_____

_____

_____

CHAPTER FOUR
The ONE LEADER Model — A New Leadership Paradigm

1. Comment on the significance of leadership being received.

2. What is the significance of the illustration about the hand in the glove? How does this describe your leadership?

3. Review the chart about Following, Serving, Influencing. How would this expand your view of leadership?

4. Describe in your own terms this inside-out growth process.

5.   How do leaders follow? Why is that important?

6.   How do leaders you know serve? How is your servanthood?

7.   Why is influencing the last yet very critical step in the process?

CHAPTER FIVE
There is One Leader and You are ... Not it!

1. Comment on what Jesus was teaching the disciples about the Pharisees and their leadership in Matthew 23.

2. What do you think Jesus means when He says there is "One Leader"?

3. As the Spirit of Jesus Christ indwells us, how does He lead through us?

4. Describe how Jesus leads from these verses from the book of John?

5. What strikes you about the phrase "Do nothing on my own initiative"?

6. How could you practically apply this verse to your leadership?

CHAPTER SIX
Brokenness and Surrender Release the Power of Christ

1. State in your own words the central idea of this chapter.

2. How is the Lord using your greatest challenges to grow as a leader?

3. How difficult is it to embrace the benefits of brokenness and surrender?

4. What is the Lord teaching you through this principle?

CHAPTER SEVEN
Following First

1. Why should following be our top priority?

2. Describe what intimacy would look like for a leader?

3. How are you doing at this?

4. Why is having a firm understanding of our identity in Christ so important?

5. How would this affect your security and significance as a leader?

6. What all comes to you when the Spirit of Christ indwells you?

7. How can you apply these three ideas of following to your leader-ship?

CHAPTER EIGHT
Leaders Serve as Second

1. What does it look like when a person aspires to be a servant leader?

2. Why is surrender so critical to the process of serving?

3. What is the connection between brokenness and surrender?

4. How does surrender affect character development?

5. How is serving connected to valuing people? What does this look like?

6. What it is the significance of having a written purpose have for a leader?

7. How does having a purpose relate to engaging in the ministry of evangelism and discipleship?

CHAPTER NINE
Influencing to the Third and Fourth Generations

1. What role do skills play in the effectiveness of a leader?

2. How do skills help leverage your influence?

3. What skills do you need the most help with?

4. Describe the team you work with or lead.

5. How and where can you apply the principles of teamwork to your situation?

6. Which one do you need to work on and why?

7. Why is having a Kingdom perspective so valuable to being a great leader?

CHAPTER TEN
Team Building – Go Fast or Go Far

1. Why are teams so important to a leader and to getting things done?

2. What situations are you facing that could use more teamwork? How?

3. What is your great challenge in developing teams?

4. What specific application can you make from this principle?

CHAPTER ELEVEN
Seek First the Kingdom

1. What is the Kingdom of God, and what significance does it play in your leadership?

2. Who are you mentoring as a next generation leader? How is this going? What are you doing?

3. How are you involved in the Great Commission?

4. Describe the legacy you are leaving.

5. What is your plan for your leadership?

CHAPTER TWELVE
Sparking a Leadership Revolution

1. What has been the most significant thing God has done as you have walked this journey?

2. How has or how will this affect your leadership?

3. What speaks to you about the example on legacy?

4. How would you describe the legacy you would like to leave behind?

5. Which of the factors on finishing well are most significant to you?

    _____

    _____

    _____

    _____

6. What did you learn about yourself from the Leadership Success Wheel? What will you work on?

    _____

    _____

    _____

7. What are you asking God for as a result of this study?

    _____

    _____

    _____

    _____

For additional help and training resources, visit LeadershipRevolution.us

ABOUT THE AUTHOR

Bruce R. Witt is President of Leadership Revolution Inc., a non-profit organization dedicated to developing and multiplying servant leaders who live as Christ and mobilize others to reach their world. He began his career in marketing for Shell Oil Company in the solid plastics area. He was led to join the Christian Business Men's Committee where he directed the U.S. field operations and authored several key curriculum for the ministry, including the Operation Timothy spiritual development series and the Lighthouse evangelism curriculum.

In 2008, after seeing the tremendous need for leaders to understand and practice Christ as the Leader in their entire life, Bruce was led to form Leadership Revolution in order to establish a process that would help leaders truly allow Christ to be their leader.

Bruce has written curriculum and training resources and he regularly travels throughout the United States and the globe conducting workshops, conferences and train the trainer sessions to spread the vision and empower others to follow Christ as their leader. Along with partner organizations and churches, Bruce has trained thousands of leaders and trained hundreds of trainers who can also train others.

Bruce has been married to his wife Dana for over 30 years and they have two grown sons, Robert and Andrew.

ABOUT LEADERSHIP REVOLUTION INC.

MISSION: To establish Christ as Leader in Every Follower.

VISION: To develop a global network of transformed leaders who lead from Christ and empower others to reach the lost and make disciples through God's power. In the next 3 years, God will work through Leadership Revolution to realize:

- *3000 leaders challenged and equipped in this unique process.*
- *300 teachers and trainers who are multiplying the process.*
- *30 partnerships with missional organizations and businesses.*

VALUES:
- *Christ is our life and leader.*
- *Leaders follow first, serve as second, and influence to the third and fourth generations.*
- *Create partner relationships with key organizations and leaders.*

LeadershipRevolution.us
678-637-9890
Bruce@LeadershipRevolution.us

JOIN US IN SHARING THE ONE LEADER

We're seeing Jesus Christ raise up leaders and change lives on five continents—North and South America, Europe, Africa, and Asia—unleashing a new generation of leaders. The need for spiritually mature leaders to reach their countries and cities with the Gospel has never been greater.

We have relationship with 16 strategic partner ministries –

Compass   •   Hoffmantown   •   Fellowship of Christian Athletes (FCA)
MELTI   •   Navigators   •   Christ Community Ministries – India
StrengthFinders   •   Ethnic America Network   •   Vision Atlanta
CBMCI   •   CBMC USA   •   Walk Thru the Bible
His Way at Work   •   ECLA (Europe)   •   FCCI   •   Life@Work

We train leaders, develop resources, and provide executive coaching to help each of the leaders to be much more effective.

Would you like to use Leadership Revolution resources and the One Leader message in your outreach? Please contact us.

LeadershipRevolution.us
678-637-9890
Bruce@LeadershipRevolution.us

THE NEXT STEP IN YOUR LEADERSHIP DEVELOPMENT

There is a crisis in our world today because of the lack of godly leaders. Leaders in business and ministry are struggling and on overload, finding themselves isolated and overly busy. We need leaders who will make a difference in the lives of people, families, and companies.

What Are You Giving Your Life To? provides a healthy dose of spiritual and practical guidance on –

- Understanding and following God's personal design and calling for you.
- How to intentionally create Kingdom-focused priorities in life and work.
- The most successful ways to overcome life's challenges and obstacles.

Start or renew your commitment to make a difference in your world.

Visit www.LeadershipRevolution.us to purchase for you or your team.